Sacred
JOURNALING

Ten Ways to Use the Power of Words
to Craft Your Ideal Life

LEILANI BARNETT

SACRED JOURNALING:
Ten Ways to Use the Power of Words to Craft Your Ideal Life
Leilani Barnett
Published by TouchPoint Press
Brookland, AR 72417
www.touchpointpress.com

ISBN: 978-1-956851-11-3

Executive Editor: Sheri Williams
Cover Painting: Ramani Urbiztondo
Cover Design: Ann Anderson Halbrooks, AMCreative

Visit the author's websites at WritingAdventures.com and LeilaniBarnett.com

@Leilani.Barnett.Author @WriterLeilani @WriterLeilani

First Edition

Printed in the United States of America.

To Jana J. Turbyfill
who encouraged me to bring journaling into my classroom
more than thirty years ago and changed my life forever

Contents

Contents

Welcome
to *Sacred Journaling*

Thank you for joining me on this journey of self-discovery! You are about to experience a universal truth, one that is both ancient and applicable to contemporary times: writing can reshape a life, help you see and change patterns, affirm the wisdom of your intuition, and set you on the path to your ideal life.

Certainly, journals are a place in which to vent safely, but they also offer a place to encourage yourself, to rewrite your script, and to rewire your thinking processes. Journaling also allows you to let go of what's not useful, beautiful, or productive and claim the best strategies, relationships, and energy to support the life you want to live. As you will see during the next few months, the practice of journaling will help you craft your ideal life.

I use the word *practice* in relation to the journaling process intentionally. Just as one *practices* magic, medicine, or law, calling forth one's deepest knowledge, so, too, does one *practice* keeping a journal, applying a combination of instinct, language, and awareness. The word *practicing* can also pertain to being engaged in pursuing a skill or way of life. One can be, for example, a *practicing* Catholic, meaning one actively engages in activities tied to a particular set of religious routines, or one can have a yoga

1

practice. Successful journaling often finds its footing in established routines and rituals. (We'll talk more about this in the pages ahead.)

Likewise, just as one can *practice* golf or participate in play *practice*, the journal accepts human imperfection, a need for ongoing work, and the implication that the practitioner is serious about doing a specific thing repeatedly. Our pages accept and challenge our weaknesses—the superficial ones like mechanical errors and the real-life ones like mishandling an important conversation. In other words, the journal not only provides a practice ground for writing, but it also becomes a place to examine one's past and rehearse one's future, to *practice*, if you will, one's own life. Your journal also provides the safest place for weighing or trying out options, for pinpointing and resolving issues, and, perhaps most importantly, for determining or affirming what it is you want to do with the precious gift that is your life.

Aiming for your ideal life, however, doesn't mean you must present yourself to your pages as a perfect being or as a perfect writer. Entries are a first draft, a free-flowing text, a place to give the page a piece of your mind. While experimentation and precision are no strangers to my journal, neither are mistakes that would send shivers up the spine of my high school English teacher. (Astoundingly, the practice of keeping a journal aids in increasing spelling and grammar skills, but that's a topic for a later chapter.) For our purpose, content alone matters when journaling.

Indeed, there is no right or wrong way to journal, although I'll offer you the best practices that have held me in good stead notebook after notebook. Most importantly, as you journal, focus on getting your thoughts on paper—period. With that said, I invite you to write and let me know how this book helps you begin to live your best life. Happy journaling!

Chapter 1: Writing You

"Start writing, no matter what.
The water does not flow until the faucet is turned on."

—Louis L'Amour, *Education of a*
Wandering Man: A Memoir[1]

When I was three years old in the late 1960s, a pretty teenager named Mona Smith babysat me. She had infinite patience, short homemade miniskirts, and a supply of pastel-colored notebook paper on which she wrote long love notes to a boy who looked a bit like young Robert Redford. To keep me out of her hair, she taught me how to spell a few words, all of which I proceeded to write on the precious pink, blue, and green paper she doled out in single sheets. I wrote my words in each of my Little Golden books, and I wrote them in crayon on a few of my mother's white walls. I fell in love with writing early, and I learned an important lesson that even fifty-three years later I refuse to debate: all the "cool kids" write. Welcome to the club!

I'm serious about having a certain bias in favor of folks of the writing ilk! My writer friends are my tribe, and my heart skips a beat whenever I spot another journal-keeper or a stranger scribbling away in an open notebook on a café table. Writers are thinkers and noticers. They understand people, emotions, and situations at a deeper level, and I find them to be among the most supportive, wise, kind, and loving people I know.

Of course, that's no coincidence! Writing fosters positive qualities as we become more reflective and as we begin to pay more attention to the world. Writing also helps us recognize and attract people who exhibit stellar qualities, traits that help them contribute to our lives in favorable ways. I'm a big fan of writers, and, therefore, a big fan of yours, because today, whether you already boast a shelf full of published books or you haven't put pen to paper since the day you left school, you are a writer.

Before you go any farther, grab a writing utensil (pen, pencil, marker, crayon) and any paper handy (the spotless notebook you just bought, the back of an electric bill, anything) and set an alarm for seven minutes. Biblically, seven is associated with wholeness and creation, and, numerologically, seven blends symbolism of the spiritual (represented by three) and the material world (represented by four), the two broad elements you'll focus on as you proceed to construct your ideal life.

For these seven sacred minutes, start writing the answer to the question that follows and keep writing without stopping to worry about spelling, punctuation, or grammar. Today, at this moment, what is compelling you to start a journal or to go deeper into your journaling? Perhaps, you recognize a desire to tell your story, an urge to live in a more authentic or satisfying way, or a wish to be an even better person than you are today. There are no right or wrong answers, and no one else ever needs to read the answers you compose. Ready? Start writing!

◆◆◆

And, just like that, you are journaling! You've now written your first entry. Feels good, huh? Sometimes, writing is like that. Whatever you said was correct. It was good enough, and so are you, by the way. Your response to the question was, in fact, perfect. The process of thinking and communicating with yourself lives and breathes in the process of journaling, but if you struggled with this first writing attempt, don't worry! The undertaking becomes easier the more you write, and you'll find you begin to look forward to—if not actually long for—the times you've set aside to put your thoughts on paper. I can't wait for you to experience the miracles journaling can produce and the magic inherent in the journaling practice.

Although journaling sounds easy and its benefits will reveal themselves to you quickly, you'll also experience times of doubt and struggle throughout this process. Trust that it is *not* self-indulgent to spend time journaling just as it is not selfish to spend time on other aspects of your health and your positive growth. In fact, journaling equates to any other spiritual practice, providing calmness, peace, and insight. Journal writing can connect us to the highest parts of ourselves, those aspects of being that remind us we are indeed created in the image of the divine. Journaling consistently helps you become the best version of yourself, and that allows you to be of maximum service to those in your world. In your journal, you may wish to spend some time reflecting on these questions: How can I serve others when I am living my ideal life? How does my presence contribute positively to those in my circle or to others in my community—even to those with whom I simply cross paths?

◆◆◆

This book offers you a menu of options—not orders or rules. As you start your first entries and the lure of the journal page begins to call, you'll find the methods, tools, and rituals that work best for you. At this time, the only rule I'm hoping you'll adopt for yourself is: just keep writing!

No one is going to grade your journal entries, judge your content, or chastise you if you should write seven minutes one day and forty-three minutes the next. Over the years, I tried other journal writers' rules, different types of guided journals, journals offering daily questions or fill-in-the-blank topics, and a plethora of subject and list suggestions. For me, starting with a date and making no more rules works best.

Within my journal, I give my instincts and intuition free reign. In fact, I don't even make myself stick to one topic when I'm journaling. Instead I often begin paragraphs with the words, "Another thing on my mind right now is . . . ." I do, however, want to make sure I exhaust my thoughts on my original topic to check that I'm not escaping a revelation I don't want to hear or make sure that I'm not avoiding a temporarily painful solution or an uncomfortable truth. Journaling is a metacognitive process; writing whatever is in your head begs you to think about your mindset. In your journal, you may wish to answer the question, "What is trending in my thoughts?" And, then answer the questions, "Why?" and "Are these thoughts productive?"

With support from these pages, which will attempt to provide you with bursts of inspiration for your writing practice—however *you* decide to implement it—you will begin to architect a journal for your purposes. In doing so you will begin to refine your life and spring to action in ways you previously thought impossible. Prepare for truths to emerge, secrets to surface, and answers to your questions to appear. Ultimately, your journal will lay the groundwork for living your most vibrant and authentic life.

◆ ◆ ◆

You may write any time of day, and you may write anywhere you find yourself. I make it a practice to buy handbags that accommodate the size of my journal. That way, I can slip writing material out in a tea shop, on a train, at work in a boring meeting, or when I'm home with a scented candle glowing in a ritualistic location like my late Grandmother Veda's roll-top desk. A kitchen table in your home or a white-clothed table in an exotic vacation spot are all the same to your journal.

Julia Cameron's classic work, *The Artist's Way*, promotes the discipline of writing three pages each morning.[2] There is much to be said for exploiting the dream time before our rational mind begins suppressing our subconscious thoughts. Still, you shouldn't limit your journaling only to morning pages in which you simply purge the contents of your mind. I've found Cameron's required page minimum assures my entries aren't superficial by forcing me to expand my initial thoughts in order to meet my self-imposed page requirements. However, I admit to having long forgiven myself for not filling a particular number of pages or meeting any other imposed requirements for my journal practice.

That said, you may wish to write in the morning for other purposes. For example, you might journal about your intentions for the day. In a broad way, you might state your goal of bringing more calmness, organization, or peace into your life. You might write about how you, as my friend, Dr. Michael Gayles, says, "Make the easy things easy." You might write about your specific priorities in various areas of your life, for instance, "Today, at work, I will . . . ," "Today for my family, I will . . . ," or maybe even, "Today to nurture myself, I will . . . ."

Morning routines—whether they relate to journaling, exercising, making one's bed, or meditating—provide a sense of accomplishment that carries through the rest of your day's activities. Journaling can be a jumpstart to a more productive twenty-four hours, a day in which you remain clear about what you want to accomplish or obtain. Each writing experience moves you one step closer to your ideal life.

◆◆◆

Conversely, an evening journal can help you reflect upon how you have spent your most precious of resources—your time! What have you accomplished? Whose day did you brighten in some small way? What did you appreciate most about this day? What would you like to re-do? In your journal, you may wish to replay a scene, examine it in detail, or rewrite it. What would you do differently? Sometimes, journals mark the activities with which we waste time rather than use time effectively for work, for service, or for relaxation. When actors flub a line the director yells, "Cut! Take two!" Journals provide a space for your daily do over, helping you rehearse to become a better, more effective actor and director within your life.

Using journals for reflection, we experience what famed diarist Anaïs Nin described as tasting life twice, "in the moment and in retrospect."[3] As we describe the significance of events, we savor the good times, freezing them like snippets of our favorite movies to be replayed again and again when we remember or read. In contrast, we also capture the times that wound us, reminding us when we are wiser or have hindsight on our side that we didn't know then what we know now. We were younger and more fragile, a state which didn't allow us to view the situation or the decision or the person with today's clarity.

Don't feel that by reflecting in your journal you wallow in the past or misuse your time in the present. Rather, you open yourself up to unlearned lessons that sharpen your sense of direction for today and tomorrow. We can't erase previous mistakes or completely eradicate the pain of past losses, but we can honor the good in our lives that chooses sometimes to visit us only briefly. We can determine what needs to change, and we can record the words and feelings, archiving our situations to review later or to use in art if we are so inclined. Our journals can become a kind of breadbox for our lives, keeping the best and worst days until we choose to take them back out and nibble on them again.

◆◆◆

You don't have to be alone every time you journal. Most recently, for example, I used my journal during a religious class. I asked a question and felt the erudite speaker avoided answering me because the reply would have shed a negative light on religious history. My emotions and thoughts were overflowing, and I felt the need to concretize and record what I was feeling, not to sweep my reality under a rug. Taking out my journal, I wrote a quick, short entry:

To be clear, Dr. ____ dismissed my question about the forced schooling of Native American children and the atrocities that took place in such schools, some of which were certainly religion-based schools. He used (fairly, I guess) my own ignorance about dates and places against me, to suppress my question, but I feel he knew exactly what I was talking about. I want to remain very certain that I am uncomfortable about the professor's unwillingness to own the damage done to people and cultures through such practices in the name of our religion. I will follow up with research on this subject myself!

Writing down my feelings in the moment helped me value and clarify myself while staying calm and present, so that I could continue to learn despite the strong feeling of being unheard. Incidentally, after the class, another participant who teaches history at a local high school came over to me and said, "I had that same question." He gave me the title of a book written by someone who had experienced such forced schooling and who wrote truthfully about the benefits and the tortures of this reality. Even if I had not been so validated by my friend,

I still owned a place in my journal, allowing me to express my experience and emotions rather than letting them overcome my ability to stay present and put the speaker's reaction in perspective. In other words, a journal can be a place to detach from a moment or experience, allowing you to separate yourself just enough to deal with it later while you instantly record the intensity, insanity, or clarity of the moment.

◆ ◆ ◆

Beware, though, that journaling can turn heads and produce an array of reactions from others. Not everyone understands journaling or other forms of writing, especially when you throw in a belief in writing's innate and ancient spiritual power, writing as a form of prayer. Perhaps I have a bit of that Biblical "no man is a prophet in his own land"[4] syndrome going on in the guise of "no woman can be a writer in her hometown," but I have found I am less self-conscious when writing in foreign cities, rather than in some beloved locations in the United States. While in Paris, for example, waiters let me be with my paper and pen unless I look up and make eye contact when I'm ready for another glass of wine or my check. There, they seem to believe, "Well, *of course*, she is writing." I sometimes feel as if there's a different level of support for writing, creating, and thinking in many other countries than there is here at home.

One night in Dublin, Ireland, where I often lead writing workshops, I was in an Italian restaurant (go figure!) and found myself without fresh pages in my journal. I asked for paper, and a waiter hurried to the cash register and then slipped me a long roll of machine tape, apologizing that he couldn't find anything else. He didn't ask *why* I needed paper. "Let me know when you need more," he said. In Ireland, it was assumed I had a thought or an experience that needed to be recorded or I had inspiration for a poem needing to be penned before the best lines slipped my mind. Likewise, when having a martini at the modern-day Hôtel de Crillon in Paris, my travel partner's request for stationery so I could write on their lovely paper as Hemingway once had was hurriedly fulfilled—no questions asked.

Of course, you can and *should* write wherever you are, but I find in Dublin and Paris, Prague or Edinburgh, Kyoto or Kigali, I feel a different level of nonchalance when I pull out my notebook to write at a table or bar. In Texas, if I pull out my journal at the hamburger joint down the street or even at my local version of a sidewalk café in Dallas, I am always prepared to meet some stares. "What is she writing in there?" I once heard someone at the next table whisper to her companion. There are extremes in Texas and Alabama, two states I've called home and states which, ironically, offer profound support for their local published authors and for the literature they produce. I'm sometimes met with a sympathetic gaze as if I'm a broken-hearted teeny-bopper writing, "Dear Diary, today Chip told me he was taking someone else to the prom." I try to smile assuredly to these strangers and send the message, "It's alright, sweetie. I'm actually having a wonderful time." The second reaction is, "I'm a writer, too! Let me tell you about my manuscript." Don't get me wrong! I've made several fine friendships in both of these situations. It just strikes me that in other locations, this seems unnecessary. Writing has wound its way into the culture in a way it simply hasn't yet in some parts of the United States. Let's change that! In your journal, make a list of places you could write within your community.

Never let someone else's response to your journaling keep you from writing when and where you want. In fact, I sometimes think of my journal as the modern-day healthy cigarette! You know, that old excuse to go outside for a bit? For sitting on a park bench in spring, for having an iced tea at a counter, for introducing yourself to someone by asking to borrow a ballpoint pen instead of a light? Writing gives me a purpose for doing something out of the ordinary in today's head down, eyes-glued-to-the-cell-phone world!

Over the years in my little corner of the planet, I have sniffed out my favorite spots to write in private and in public—the cute restaurant with the vine-covered cedar pergola, the landmark restaurant with a friendly bartender and a famous Texas Sunset cocktail, the fireplace seating in a fancy lobby of a hotel I couldn't afford twenty years ago, or the dark, candle-lit church with its open doors every afternoon between masses. Find your writing sweet spots; wandering is as much a part of the writing adventure as wondering!

Wherever I am, journaling allows me to meet other writers, philosophers, artists, and thinkers. My journal has become the red carnation worn on blind dates in years past. It has become my calling card or letter of introduction from the Victorian Period or the Gilded Age. It says to others who understand the journaling process: I'm one of you, using my words to grapple with the human condition and to make sense of life as I know it.

There will never be a better time to honor yourself and those around you by taking out a paper and pen. This time is all we have. Whatever you do, start writing. You may wish to answer my favorite question from my friend Laura Bridwell-Meyeres, which is, "So, what's *really* going on?" or my favorite teaching question, not "Do you have any questions?" but instead, "What questions do you have?" You may wish to simply write freely, letting the thoughts flow in a stream-of-conscious fashion. Ease the pressure if you find the blank page daunting by continuing to set your timer for seven minutes and giving yourself permission to stop when the buzzer signals you've met your goal. You might find you want to continue writing, and if so, that's perfectly fine!

Lysette Flores, former Director of Campus Ministry for Bishop Lynch High School, told me a story about the Christmas her father, "a man of few words," gave all the children in her family their own diaries. In each, he'd written a special note. "Through the gift, he invited us to write about our lives," Flores explained. "He admitted that he wished he had recorded more during his lifetime." Consider this book your invitation to write about your life. Give yourself permission to record and examine and dream in the pages of your notebook.

As a college composition instructor, I once taught an older student whose first writing dealt with the death of a favorite cousin. They were children, crossing a road, when the youngster let go of the other's hand and walked forward into the pathway of an oncoming car. The writing was wrought with agony and guilt. During a conference at the end of the class in which the student had continued to pen other academic essays with precision and vividness, he said, "I have never wanted to write before now. If I hadn't written down my cousin's story, I don't think I could have written anything this year." His memory of this traumatic event laid in wait for him whenever he faced the open arms of a blank page. By confronting the memory and recording it, his mind was free to concentrate on other less emotionally charged topics.

Like my student, you might have a long-held story, biding its time, waiting to be released, or you might want to fill a journal page with a list of all the memories you never want to talk about. But, if that is simply too unsettling or you'd like to start with an easier topic, you may wish to start with something requiring little or no emotional investment, such as "This morning at breakfast . . .," assuming the meal was, indeed, a somewhat uneventful meal. As you start, the point of journaling is to get words on paper.

You might even start with a description of how you view yourself as a writer. Do you have a preconceived notion of what writers and journal keepers are like? What stereotypes do you bring to the idea of The Writer? How would you describe the part of you seeking to express yourself? Most importantly, how do you predict writing will change your life?

Chapter 2: Mistake-Proof You

"What will I write in this beautiful book? She carried the book
to class for the rest of the day, and that night she put it
under her pillow, still blank. She liked it blank right now,
liked to know that it was waiting, listening. Just like her friends."

—Simone St. James, *The Broken Girls*[5]

Being mistake-proof doesn't mean you never make mistakes; it means you embrace them as the lessons they are or as benchmarks along the path toward your ultimate success. They don't break you. Mistakes don't ruin a journal, and they don't ruin a life. I am a sucker for the ornate bound journals one finds in stationery stores and museum gift shops. Friends and students have gifted me many over the years, and I've collected others from places I've traveled. For a long time, I didn't write in these aesthetically pleasing books. I didn't want to make mistakes or have cross outs in these too-pretty-to-use notebooks. Now, I do. I realize my journal entries *are* important enough to deserve such fancy settings, because I've witnessed the extraordinary changes and experienced new levels of awareness and appreciation that writing brings to my life.

It's not the writing itself that is worthy, but the actions, the requests for forgiveness, the intentions, and decisions spurred on by journaling that deserve the pages of sumptuous blank books. I suspect it also has much to do with the way my thinking about mistakes has changed over the years, the way I've accepted imperfections, scars, and obstacles as inevitable and valuable parts of life's journey. Mistakes *are* essential, and this is not only true for life in general but also for writing. When you free yourself from worrying about errors, poor spelling, sentences that aren't exactly parallel, and commas that don't land in the right place, you focus on the meaning of content. That is the meat of a journal!

Surprisingly, almost three decades of using journaling with students proved to me that a year of daily writing does more to improve one's sentence structure, diction, grammar, and spelling than a hundred drills or diagramming exercises! Don't worry about mechanical skills as you write, just put thoughts on paper as well as you can. Improvement comes, as it usually does, with practice and experimentation, not by putting your attention on being correct.

Once I worked with a student writer who had learned early in life that if she kept her sentences dull and short, she wouldn't have to worry about the teacher's red pen finding her errors. Even before beginning her bland, safe writing, she would stare at the empty pages for a long time and keep the white correction fluid handy. If she managed to write during our class, she would write a sentence or two and need immediate reassurance from me that she hadn't made a mistake. "Can you check this? Am I doing this right?" she asked.

Finally, after one such incident, I took the student's paper and said, "Now, I'm going to do something shocking. Don't panic!" Then, I took her paper, gently wadded it up in a ball, and unfolded it to reveal new creases that refused to come out. I tore a bit here and there, made a random pencil mark or two, and then I handed the paper back to her. "Now, it's not perfect. You can make as many mistakes as you want on this page." She was aghast at first, but then she laughed and took her messed-up paper to her desk where she proceeded to create a fascinating and dynamic piece of writing, quite different from the error-free but sleep-inducing assignments she previously turned in.

Similarly, just as a mistake-free life doesn't challenge or intrigue us, writing like that doesn't allow us permission to focus on our thoughts. Instead we concentrate on potential errors which leads to dullness, dryness, and lack of growth and honesty. If we always play it safe, we miss some amazing adventures. And if we do so in our writing, we miss the truth and the wisdom that come with taking risks.

I've met only a few people whose hearts haven't been broken yet, people who haven't hit rock bottom through no fault of their own, people who have never suffered an almost unbearable loss, or those whose rises to success have been quick and easy. When I have met such charmed folks, I didn't quite trust their judgment because they don't yet know who they are. They also don't know who *you* are because they lack the empathy experience fosters. Until you have faced challenges that flatten you, how do you know you have the spirit to pull yourself up?

For example, in the blissful ignorance of youth, I believed I had and would always have Superwoman energy, the ability to juggle multiple projects simultaneously, and the answers to most questions. I'd also not yet been gutted by betrayal nor watched a fairytale life evaporate overnight. I had not yet been handed a pink slip as my reward for having stood up against a racist and sexist boss a decade before the eras of the Me Too movement or Black Lives Matter. I had not yet realized I'd spent a year watering someone else's field instead of taking care of my own emotional and professional gardens. I've met many young people who are endowed with humility and maturity beyond their years, but for me, it took some time to realize mistakes can carry you to the high points just as quickly as doing everything right.

According to *How to Think Like Leonardo da Vinci: Seven Steps to Genius Every Day* by Michael J. Gelb, one of the principles adopted by the great artist, inventor, and philosopher was *dimostrazione* or "a commitment to test knowledge through experience, persistence, and a willingness to learn from mistakes."[6] Mistakes aren't just unavoidable; they are necessary for growth and discovery. Accepting the inevitability of errors, false starts, and brick walls doesn't mean you'll run into them painlessly, but it does bring a sense of receptivity to their lessons.

◆◆◆

Despite my being comfortable with marring expensive or beautiful journals, my favorite book in which to write is a wide-lined composition notebook, the kind sold at discount stores for less than a dollar. I glue on a collage of pictures from magazines or travel advertisements or use construction paper shapes to create a unique cover. I then use clear packing tape around the front to secure and waterproof the front and back of my book. These books are lightweight, fit the size of my handwriting perfectly, and don't seem to put much pressure on me to be perfect!

The colors you choose for your ink or your notebook cover can reinforce your intentions. As with other earth elements, colors promote particular feelings and energies. Psychiatrists, priests, and interior decorators alike can agree on some general color associations, but what is most important as you choose colors to decorate your journal will be the meanings *you* attribute to each tint, tone, or shade. For instance, I sometimes mindfully eat an orange—a quick charm for when I feel writer's block or become stuck in any other creative endeavor or personal situation. The citrus smell along with the bright, fresh color puts me in a different frame of mind, exuding an energy which aids my creativity.

Bowls of oranges, apricots, and peaches provide instant remedies for times when the writing, thoughts, or solutions aren't flowing effortlessly. They are also messy fruits, and allowing the juice to run down my fingers and onto blank pages reminds me to let go of any perfectionist tendencies keeping me from writing or stopping me from taking action in my life. I associate the color orange with the funniest, weirdest, most friendly parts of myself. The parts that attract the right people, characters, lines, or ideas are associated with the color orange, along with innovation and social relationships.

I use purple when I'm working on boosting my sense of self-worth. As a royal color, as the same shade chosen by Vice President Kamala Harris on her inauguration day to represent unity, and as a color promoting the energy of intuition, a tinge of purple's strength on or within your journal will help connect you with what your wisest self already knows. I incorporate blue when desiring more peace in my life, black when I feel the need for protection, and red when I want renewed interest. Red, for me, eliminates or invigorates anything I find lackluster. It might sound silly, but try it. If you are writing in red ink, it's difficult to write about the mundane. There are many sources for expanding your knowledge on the way the brain and body respond to color. For now, select and employ the color or colors calling to you as you begin to choose or to decorate a notebook to become your first sacred journal.

◆ ◆ ◆

Whether it's the inexpensive book I decorate myself or a book with handmade paper and a rich leather cover, I prefer some kind of bound book for writing. When I find myself without a journal, I write on loose-leaf paper and simply fold those sheets and later staple or tape them into my journal. Author and writing guru, Natalie Goldberg advocates for cheap spiral notebooks,[7] but when I travel, I often opt for a sturdy Moleskine notebook with its handy pocket in the back. The latter is an ideal size for most purses, backpacks, or briefcases. When my travel includes a workshop or training, I choose to use a sketchbook as my journal, one large enough to hold maps, postcards, business cards, and the addresses of new friends, plus, of course, some rudimentary sketches and lots of writing.

My father and my grandfather both kept a tiny notepad in the pockets of their Western shirts. They were not journal writers as far as I know, but the memo pad was handy for jotting down ideas or reminders. I, too, keep a second pocket-size journal as it fits snugly into a cocktail purse. I don't want to be without something to write on when I'm inspired at a symphony, a museum, or even a rodeo. You never know when you will overhear a piece of dialogue or see a scene or a piece of art you want to revisit later in your writing or reflecting.

Once during a particularly dramatic moment of an opera I was attending with another writer friend, David Roberts, a woman in front of us began slumping onto her spouse's shoulder. It became clear she had passed out or passed on. We didn't know which as an usher called an ambulance and paramedics arrived, placing the lifeless woman on a stretcher and then rushing her away—all while the symphony played on, getting louder and louder, and as the singers moved closer and closer to the front of the stage, their voices ringing throughout the hall. No doubt, our journals that evening contained our contemplations about the irony of the real-life scene juxtaposed with the equally dramatic Verdi opera, which continued even as the couple faced a potentially true-life tragedy. Writing boxes up scenes for you to use later in your own writing or to reflect upon as a mini lesson thrown at you by life. When writing such things, does it matter whether your journal costs fifty cents or fifty dollars?

Your journal can be an expression of your personality and interests or just a container for your writing. Experiment. You'll find the tools that feel right!

◆◆◆

As I sit here, typing away, the obvious question comes to mind—can one journal on a laptop or other electronic device? Of course, some writers prefer a keyboard. I like to type non-fiction chapters and articles, but there is something more magical and sacred about handwriting, something more authentic and revealing. When I've experimented with keeping a journal via my laptop, I've not found it as satisfying as seeing the thoughts emerge in my own penmanship. A handwritten journal entry reflects me more significantly.

There's a whole field of professional handwriting analysts who make their living explaining patterns of our marks on the page, the loops and swoops, the tight letters, or blank spaces. Such components, these graphologists insist, connect to personality characteristics, revealing whether we hide jealousy or generosity, shyness, confidence, dependability, or a tendency to be flighty. A number of corporations even hire professional analysts to take part in the hiring process, noting the degree of the writer's slant, how the potential employee uses space between words or letters, and the amount of force she or he uses to press down the writing instrument.

I'm not suggesting that you analyze your handwriting in your journal, although I find it a fun exercise. However, in terms of journaling, I do believe in the science behind graphology. The physical orders your brain gives to your arms and hands to complete the muscular movements necessary to create writing are controlled by the central nervous system. These movements, and thus your handwriting itself, can be affected by your emotions, by the extent to which the ego is at work, and even by the stiffness or relaxation you are experiencing. All said, the end result means your handwriting is a true extension of you, of all that you are experiencing and all that you are trying to express or trying to hide away!

Equally important, using a computer gives you the opportunity to erase your mistakes, and mistakes, my friend, are valuable insights you might wish to consider later. Keep your erasers and liquid correction pens away from your journal. There's nothing wrong with a mark out. My journalism professor, Keith Cannon, taught me to use a simple editing mark, a single line ending with a small, neat loop that looks like the letter *e* drawn through the word, letter, or phrase I wish to delete. If I had a dollar for each of those marks that found its way into my journal. . . . Ah well! They served their purpose, which was to give me permission to U-turn, back up, or simply be wrong.

Handwriting is certainly slower than typing, but part of the point of journaling *is* to slow down, giving yourself time to contemplate, express your thoughts, question or clarify them, and to mark the significance of events, not just log them as a diary. Those of us who grew up in the age of friendly letters remember our teachers and mentors who stressed the importance of handwriting personal letters and thank you notes. It was considered poor manners and impersonal to type such missives. Typing was taking the easy way out. It was a degree of separation between you and the recipient of your message. In similar fashion, a keyboard provides a mask of sorts, a distance between you and the page. Embrace your handwriting—good, bad, or ugly—and look forward to writing authentic, mistake-laced journals!

◆ ◆ ◆

As a youngster, I sat in my father's shop where he crafted leather belts, wallets, purses, and even gun holsters. He hand-tooled them with ornate Western designs. I can still smell the leather as he selected the perfect implement out of his neatly arranged collection of chrome-plated stamps, punches, skivers, swivel cutters, and rounded knives. Several of his pieces are in my home today. I didn't inherit the craftsmanship that marked his leatherworking, but I did learn from him the importance of having the right tool for the right job. Perhaps, this is why I make no apologies for spending time in this book to talk about the tools involved in journaling.

Inevitably, security-minded sales people surround me on the floor of office supply stores when I wander into the pen section. They seem puzzled and suspicious at the time I spend browsing, holding, sniffing, and trying out their wares. "What's she up to?" they seem to ask themselves after the first twenty minutes or so. You can grab any writing instrument you have on hand and begin to journal, but pencil marks fade with time and ballpoints require more force on the page than the pens I recommend. To me, the writing instrument you choose matters, which is not to say you should wait until you've purchased that Montblanc to begin to journal! I admit though, I treasure one I received as a gift coupled with blue-black ink that makes my handwriting resemble those in vintage letters my great-aunts might have written. In my purse, you'll find a black Precise V7 rolling ball, fine, not very fine, which Pilot also offers as an option. No matter how much I write, I never find my hand or wrist in pain as I sometimes do with cheaper pens.

On an airplane or for trips overseas, I opt for the Uni-Ball Vision Elite rollerball pens, which, like the V7, come full of a deep black ink that flows out smoothly, always reminding me of Rebecca's signature in the Daphne du Maurier novel. For much less than the cost of a fancier fountain pen, the Uni-ball also offers its own version of blue-black ink, but its major claim to fame is not bursting in flight! Like the Precise V7, the Uni-ball remains easy on the wrist when you write for long periods, and it doesn't make your hand ache even when you're at your most fluent and productive. Uni-balls are a staple in the swag bags I give writers who participate in my Writing Adventures workshops abroad, and on my packing list they are second only to an up-to-date passport.

◆ ◆ ◆

Just as my love of paper and pens goes back to my early childhood, so does my love of other readers and writers. Reading and writing make us more compassionate and empathetic, and we increase our understanding of our effect on others as we reflect on how we respond to people in our lives. As we become more aware and accepting of our mistakes and flaws, so too do we become more tolerant of the mistakes of others. In other words, writers in general make lovely friends, and I've surrounded myself with these forgiving noticers. They prove to me that writing makes you more tolerant, not just of your own shortcomings but of the people around you.

Growing up in a small town meant living under a microscope. Gossip rivaled Friday night football as the most popular local sport, and instead of "because I said so," the answer I received to "Why can't I?" was more often, "because people will talk about you." I still believe in personal morality that takes as its cornerstone, mercy, acceptance, love, and a desire to do no harm to anyone else, but as an adult I have given up on the question, "What will they think?" Some of the best advice I ever got came from my childhood next-door neighbor and high school physical science teacher, Andy Jones, who told me, "Some people are going to like you no matter what. Some people won't like you no matter what." No matter what you do or say or how you dress or behave, some people will approve of your choices and some won't. Perfection isn't possible by everyone else's standards, but healthy growth is always a worthy goal. Journaling can help you continue to discern between the two. These days, I focus not on the question of "Why doesn't this person like me?" or "What will people think about this?" and instead focus on "How can I improve?" and "Am I happy with this choice or with who I am today?"

◆ ◆ ◆

Many years ago, I had the opportunity to attend a graduate course in Romantic-era poetry with the brilliant and versatile astronaut, Story Musgrave. As a quiet twenty-something who cared about her grades, I was terrified when our professor stated that if he remembered we didn't speak up in class and express our opinions, he would not give us an A even if our written work justified a perfect grade. So, one day after the professor had asked Musgrave about his opinion of a Blake poem, I seized my opportunity to share a contrasting interpretation.

I argued ferociously for my viewpoint as the professor and Musgrave listened patiently to my voice become almost angry-sounding while my hands began to shake with each new piece of evidence I presented. I was as scared speaking in class that day as I would have been stepping out into space from a shuttle, something I later watched Musgrave do as I was watching a national news program. It wasn't the public speaking of which I was afraid; I feared being wrong and I worried that smarter students would reveal it and revel in my wrongness. What a gift and a lesson it was when Musgrave, asked by the professor if he wanted to respond to my criticism, declined to invalidate my observations as he might easily have done and simply shrugged and said, "I could be wrong."

I hadn't known that was an option! What a paradigm-shifting moment! In the future, I began to speak my mind more easily and less confrontationally in classes and in other situations, but my most productive conversations have been those when I opened myself to being wrong or to simply not having a clue! I began to learn to listen and to say, "What do you think?" and to share my notions with a more comfortable relationship to potential wrongness. Journaling helped me not only understand the lesson of that classroom event, but to continue to

24

apply it as I asked myself in many circumstances, "If I'm wrong, what would another alternative be?" or "How might I think or justify an opposite opinion?" or "How can I respond graciously to others who believe or think differently than I do?"

Having grown up in a community of only 1,500 people, surrounded by the same citizens most of whom were part of similar religious congregations, I remember being quizzed about my church leanings by a new friend whose life had been less sheltered and whose experiences and reading had been broader than my own. "Did you ever think," he asked curiously, "that you might be wrong?" No, I responded, I never had. That wasn't faith on my part, that was small mindedness or simple ignorance. Experiencing the mystery of faith and being spiritual sojourners whether we describe ourselves as Catholics or Cynics, Protestants or Pagans, does not require that we blindly follow leaders or teachings or doctrine. To grow spiritually or emotionally, we have to be willing to say, "I might be wrong. I might not know everything." In fact, many great religious leaders, including Christ, have modeled for us a willingness to sit at the feet of teachers. Whether we find ourselves in a temple or a classroom, let's open our minds and our journals and ask, "About what could I be wrong?" Ask, "What are some things I believe to be true, and why do I believe what I believe? How would life change if I were wrong about something I now believe profoundly?" Examine closely the consequences of being wrong. What would it mean to you if you were wrong about something important or even something small? What are your fears around the issue of making a mistake or not being correct? Would any mistakes truly ruin your life or simply change its course?

◆◆◆

It has become almost a cliché to champion the idea that mistakes are opportunities for learning and growth, but that doesn't dilute the truth of the statement. What mistakes do you need to revisit in order to learn? Give them some time in your journal. For what do you need to forgive yourself or others? What unchangeable elements do you think of as flaws that could possibly be reframed as positives? What expectations did others have for you that didn't match your own desires? Do you need to forgive yourself for following a path someone else set out for you or realize that you are responsible for how you respond to all that happens to you from this point on? You might start, "I forgive myself for not living up to the expectation of . . . ." You might start by pondering what mistake you wish you had made or something you would like to do that might turn out to be a mistake.

One of the saddest stories I've ever read is "Eveline" found in James Joyce's *Dubliners*.[8] A young woman wants to step out of her current life, leave her sometimes brutal family of origin, and travel with the man of her dreams, but at the last minute she finds herself rooted to the ground, clinging to the bland familiar. She can't bring herself to risk a potential mistake. What foolish things have you avoided that might have brought more joy into your life? What have you learned from your biggest mistake? What mistake do you want to make next?

Chapter 3: Free You

"Freedom is nothing but a chance to be better."

—Albert Camus, *Conférences et Discours* [9]

In Chaucer's *The Canterbury Tales*, the Wife of Bath shares a quest story in which a disgraceful knight seeks the answer to the question, "What do women most want?"[10] At the end of his journey, a magical crone supplies the correct answer as wizened witches have a tendency to do—women want sovereignty over their own lives. We women and we writers want what all humans want—the freedom to do what we want. Certainly, American culture values freedom. "Land of the free"[11] we claim to be. In fact, as I write these words, protesters are dumbfounding many of us as they rail against reasonable shelter-in-place orders designed to keep our citizens safe from a deadly pandemic, because whether simply misguided and stir crazy or acting out of economic desperation, the protesters claim, they want their "freedom." Car advertisements, travel brochures, and adolescents on their way to becoming young adults tout the desirability of freedom. Surely, freedom is more than being able to collect stamps in a passport, to risk a deadly illness to get a haircut, or to get out from under the watchful eye of a caring parent.

Journaling has helped me examine the concepts of freedom, permission, and living in ways I might otherwise have missed in the busy every day way of life. Writing about my experiences and people I have met allowed me to come to a realization that most of us live the majority of our lives according to someone else's script. By exploring the idea of freedom in my journal, I've realized that for the lion's share of us, the outline we follow is self-imposed. Never has this been clearer to me than when I purchased a house. It was a lovely suburban home nestled under a protected mountain in Northeast Alabama, and it had all the room I needed or would ever need. The reality, though, was I simply wasn't a "house person" at that time. I enjoyed being downtown more than being tucked away from restaurants, pubs, and theaters. The lawn, alone, consumed me. I preferred reading a novel or watching a classic movie on television to trimming hedges or mowing grass. Furthermore, the rooms for which I now paid were not necessary, and as I was a zealous traveler, the heavy mortgage cut into my vacation fund. Why then did I believe this was the decision for me?

Simple answer: My husband and I had tried to live by a script meant for a more conventional couple, people with more children and fewer travel dreams, those who took pride in a freshly cut lawn, those whose art was less controversial, those who hadn't memorized the menu of every restaurant in our city. Friends, family, and even our tax preparer, however, advised us to get a house. "Having an apartment is just throwing away money," they told us, but for us living in a rented apartment would have given us freedom, freedom from the chores we despised, from the responsibility of fixing things that broke along the way, from the time-consuming tasks that ate up our lives in ways we didn't enjoy. The script was, "People your age and in your professions purchase homes in the suburbs," and we followed the script to our detriment.

The house versus apartment battle represents just one kind of script that can be confining, making us feel that we don't have freedom. The reality is we have much more liberty than we allow ourselves to enjoy! "We're supposed to . . ." is not a reason to make a decision that doesn't fit us. My favorite question for people who tell me, "I wish I could . . ." is "Well, why can't you?" You might be wondering, "What does the idea of embracing your freedom have to do with journaling?" Well, the more we journal the better we know ourselves and the better we can choose pathways, professions, homes, and relationships that fit us. In other words, the more we journal the more permission we give ourselves to begin making the decisions that lead us directly to our ideal lives.

A frequent exercise I use in my journal is to begin with "I wish I had the freedom to . . . ." Then, I follow up by writing about why I want to do or have the things or experiences I've identified. I set out my motivations and then set about to find solutions within my uncensored writing. In my journal, I'm not hindered by critics who would say, "Oh, that wouldn't work" or "You can't do that the way you want." No one sighs, shakes his head, rolls her eyes, or suppresses a giggle when I dream in my journal. I simply produce the magic words of my wishes and don't worry about knocking down obstacles.

In your journal, ask yourself to identify scripts you follow though they no longer serve you. What rules have you been taught regarding what it means to be a good person that really don't make sense? For example, are there things you are not allowed to do? Things that in their avoidance don't make you a more devout or disciplined person, more ethical and kinder, more close to the higher power? What rules have you accepted or made for yourself about how to live what mainstream society or your particular community would consider a 'normal' (as if there is anything!) life? How could you liberate yourself from some of the frameworks for living that don't fit with your passions and dreams? Did you have any childhood fantasies about your adult life that you haven't yet made come true? What's your next step to make those dreams realities? Begin an entry with the words, "I give myself permission to . . . ."

◆ ◆ ◆

Continue using the journal to rid yourself of 'shouldn't' stories. I have friends who have been told they shouldn't be gay, shouldn't be single or married, shouldn't own so many pets, shouldn't run marathons, shouldn't give money to this or that charity. Perhaps you have been told you shouldn't explore a vegan diet, a travel itch, an acting bug, or law school. I have been told that I shouldn't travel to Rwanda, France, Mexico, New Zealand, or Japan—places where I have met charming, helpful people who enriched my life. As a public school teacher, I was told I shouldn't care about my salary, that I shouldn't expect much from my students, and that I shouldn't count on kids to read or write too much. I've challenged each of these pieces of advice with positive results.

A simple burning ritual works wonders to eradicate these not-so-helpful stories, allowing us to free ourselves from the power of doubt as smoke wafts skyward. Think about a time when someone has poured cold water on a dream or desire you expressed, or consider a time when your own mind or inner killjoy filled you with self-doubt, making you wonder what others would think or whether or not others would be bothered or angry about your decisions. Jot down some key words related to the incident and then tear the paper into the smallest pieces possible and safely burn. Then, pray for a new and better story, asking that doubts in your own abilities transform into new confidence. Think to yourself, as the smoke dissipates, so too are the thoughts that held me down. As the memories and engrained patterns I've written on paper are destroyed, so too is the power of the convenient, the known, and the comfortable demolished and forever felled. Breathe in new freedom to be the person you were created to be, to do what you want to do with the companions you choose to share your journey.

♦ ♦ ♦

The entire process of keeping a journal is a microcosm of fashioning a lifestyle filled with less oppression and more freedom. Between the covers of your journal, you create your own world. In the previous chapter, you were encouraged not to be intimidated or silenced by preconceived notions of perfection as you compose journal entries. Exploring your idea of what being a writer means might uncover even more misconceptions of which you can let go. Are you a powerful career woman "too busy" to write? My friend Julie Wilkerson showed me that wasn't true as she wrote in airports and hotels while traveling from America to Asia for business. Do you believe you are too young to have experiences worth writing about? Mary Shelley began writing *Frankenstein* when she was nineteen, and Willa Cather assured us that "most of the basic material" a writer needs for fodder is gathered "before the age of fifteen."[12,13]

Perhaps you think you are too old to start a new writing practice? Well, Millard Kaufman was ninety when he published his first book, *Bowl of Cherries*,[14] and Harriet Doerr won the National Book Award for *Stones of Ibarra*,[15] a book published when she was seventy-four years old. Certainly, the list of authors who have published their first works in their forties, fifties, and sixties is long and illustrious, containing the likes of Raymond Chandler, Toni Morrison, and Marcel Proust—proving it's never too late to let memory flow through your pen. Moreover, most of the poetry of Wallace Stevens was written after his late fifties. Can you imagine the loss of "Thirteen Ways of Looking at a Blackbird,"[16] for example, had Stevens thought, "Oh, forget it! I'm a retired executive, not a poet!" Imagine what beautiful moments, observations, and ideas will be lost if we let our perception of what journal writers "should" be like hamper our ability to create.

Likewise, I mentioned the importance of not being abashed by memories of a teacher's red pen. As you release fears about expressing yourself and think more closely about your life and how you want to spend this time on our planet, you'll be practicing the very method you'll use to take more responsibility for your environment, your job, your relationships, and even your financial situation. In short, as you take control of this activity—taking out a notebook and writing in it frequently—you experience a preview of how you can take control of other spaces in your world. The power of your words becomes contagious, spreading to other areas in your life, as if with your pen you are casting a spell for success that spills over from one area to the next.

Journaling reminds you that you are a self-determining being. Jack Canfield's *The Success Principles: How to Get from Where You Are to Where You Want to Be* starts with the revelation that "there is only one person responsible for the quality of the life you live,"[17] and it's not your parents, your boss, your spouse, or anyone else! You, Canfield advises, must take 100% responsibility for your life. As you write each day, you will, no doubt, use your pages for venting frustrations and strong emotions, but you'll find the process more liberating if you keep in mind that only your responses and decisions enslave you to any particular way of life.

Canfield's philosophy at first glance might seem a heavy burden to bear. Not having anyone else to blame for where you find yourself . . . ouch! However, I have found claiming responsibility is liberating. My journal acts as a mirror and advisor, reminding me as I document my thoughts that much *is* within my control, especially how I respond to circumstances, to people, to negativity, and to obstacles.

◆ ◆ ◆

Go far enough down into your subconscious and you might find attached to the word *freedom* the word *reckless*. We might envision the train-hopping vagabond or the lonely cowboy drifting into the sunset. We might hear Janis Joplin's voice, echoing "Me and Bobby McGee."[18] Freedom can be scary. If there are no plots to follow, what will you do? If there are no limits on your dreams, what might you do? How far will you go? A little voice whispers, "Is that *too* far?" As you begin to embrace the reality that your destiny lies in your hands, it becomes time to reflect upon the fears associated with success. It is time to confront old messages and old ways of thinking that could hold you back from crafting the perfect life.

What are your self-imposed rules? They can be harmless, of course, like stubbornly adhering to the "right way" of folding towels, even if it means refolding laundry with which someone else has helped. But the rules we accept as the only possibilities can also be damaging, like believing everyone has to get married or have children to be completely fulfilled when those lifestyles aren't your true desires.

My favorite poem by Kaylin Haught features a speaker asking God if it's "okay to be melodramatic," "to be short," to "wear nail polish or not," and the answer? Well, God ends the conversation by saying, "Sweetcakes [. . .] / what I'm telling you is / Yes Yes Yes."[19] I love that poem. I love the fact that glorious permission comes when you realize the purpose of a divine entity who loves us is surely not out to corral us into neat little boxes or to make all the characters march the same plotline. How would our perceptions and actions change if we really believed that God wants only to love us? We *choose* so many of our 'shoulds'— and not necessarily for our own good or even the good of those we love, but because we have been brought up on a script or told a story about what we are supposed to want and what we are supposed to do and not do.

As an academic coach, I've often had to convince new teachers that they don't have to teach particular texts, use an outdated method, or become replicas of their own high school teachers. Acknowledging this freedom has allowed these young instructors to make their lessons more relevant to their students' interests. "It never occurred to me," one teacher said, "that I didn't have to do things the same way the teacher before me did!" I continue to feel that same astonishment at myself when I realize I have failed to buck a system that isn't best serving those I love or me. Traditions can be empowering and renewing but saying, "This is how it's done" or "but, we've always done it this way" doesn't necessarily lead to a life that is effective and enjoyable. Just as new medical treatments come along that make doctors better able to take care of us, new methods, new opportunities, and new ways of thinking and living come along to make us better human beings, more akin to the divine purpose for which we were all created as unique individuals.

Dare to make a small change today that lets you grab more joy and less stress by being just a tiny bit different from other people you know. For heaven's sake, don't let your predictions about what other people might think cloud your judgment! Who cares if your child's kindergarten teacher sees you in an older model car that still runs well if not trading up allows you to take fabulous trips abroad each year? Who cares if you wear velvet after February 14, a rule I picked up during my years in the deep South, or if your purse doesn't match your shoes but is perfect for carrying your painted water bottle or your fabulous new journal? Who cares if you wear black every day or don your spring colors in the throes of winter? We will all be judged, and we all harbor a predisposition for judging. Let's ask ourselves in our journals to identify the origin of these judgments, especially those that keep us from accepting and loving others and ourselves as well as we should.

Use your journal to help you break through the barrier of the giant misconception that you must do something in a particular way in order to be successful or happy. What would your life look like without all the rules or traditions you've not chosen for yourself? How would having all the money you need change your priorities? When you explore these questions in your journal and find your answers, ask yourself, "How can I change my life now to live as I would if money were not an issue?"

In what ways have you been on autopilot, tiptoeing around the life you want but never truly embracing it? In your journal make a vow to yourself that from this day forward, you will make deliberate decisions about how you spend your time and money. You'll never taste freedom living a life someone else designed! Your journal can be a sacred template for the full, sparkling life intended for you.

In Sandra Cisneros' beautiful little collection of vignettes, *The House on Mango Street*, Esperanza's aunt advises her to keep writing. "Writing," the sickly woman confined to bed tells her niece, "will keep you free."[20] There, in my opinion, has never been a statement containing a greater amount of truth.

Chapter 4: Secret You

"There are no secrets time does not reveal."

—Jean Racine, *Britannicus*[21]

When I was about three, my mother had taken me with her to Turner's Dry Goods in my hometown and purchased a pair of new work boots for my dad. Martha Woods had wrapped them beautifully, and Mother and I went straight home and placed the box under the Christmas tree. "Don't tell Daddy!" Mother warned me, but by the time my father arrived home from work at 5:15 p.m. I guess I had forgotten her admonition. "Take off your old boots, Daddy," I cried, handing him the box, "and put on your new boots!" It wasn't the first or last time I've ruined a holiday surprise!

I'm still not good at keeping secrets, and I will never be a poker player. Even if I manage not to say what I'm thinking, my face often reveals my feelings. I've had to learn to assume blank affect when interviewing others or when the grandchildren say funny, cute things at which I should not laugh. A confidence

I can keep, but a surprise is entirely different. Journaling allows me to consider what I want to tell, how I want to tell it, who I want to tell it to, and what the results of sharing that information could be.

Journals are an almost perfect confidante. They do not talk to others, but they reflect back to us anything we are willing to see. Our thoughts on paper can seem new to us. "How do I know what I think until I see what I say?" asked Graham Wallas.[22] Flannery O'Connor agreed, saying she wrote because, "I don't know what I think until I read what I say."[23] By journaling, you aren't just keeping a log of the thoughts you have; the act of writing spawns fresh thinking and original ideas.

If you're new to journaling, you might ask, "But wouldn't a conversation with a trusted friend accomplish the same thing?" It could, and it might, but human confidantes have human limitations. By thinking on paper even before confiding in others you can determine what you want to share, how much you want to share, and why you want to share that information. Within your journal, you can show all sides of yourself, and you can do so without censoring, skewing, or wondering how the listener is going to respond.

With the help of a journal, you can sometimes control the reveal of information, either of the deep, dark variety or the typical human feelings and experiences. For example, if I consider a new position, I might admit to my journal that I'm motivated in large part by the salary increase, but if I share this information with a colleague, he or she might repeat it. To those making the hiring decisions, this honest statement might be spun into "She only cares about the money." However, in a journal, I could consider all aspects of why I want the job, such as the appealing challenges and those with which I feel uncomfortable, the pros and cons of leaving one position and taking another, what might be motivating me to desire professional change. Then, I can determine if, when, how, and with whom I want to share that information.

What is your history with secrets? Have you revealed too much, spilled the beans about a surprise, or lifted the lid off a confidence? What were the reactions or long-term effects? Were relationships changed, and if so, was the relationship spoiled or made stronger? Conversely, has anyone ever broken your trust? How did you respond? Would you respond differently now? Journal pages don't have loose lips and are, therefore, the perfect place to unpack the secrets that hold us back and decide what real-life situations and people warrant knowing our darkest fears, our deepest desires, and our strongest doubts.

We don't have to consider the audience when writing in a journal. Today, social media platforms tempt us to present our most perfect versions of ourselves for the consumption of our friends, family, colleagues, and even acquaintances. Our pictures are edited, filters can be used to make us more attractive, and the negative incidents with which we have dealt can be omitted in what we share. You post your smiling family, opening their holiday gifts, and not the argument you had with your husband's ex-wife about which of you would get Christmas morning with the children. We don't tell how disappointed our son was not to get an expensive video game we couldn't afford that year or how relieved we were when family finally went home, the tree was down, and life was back in order. I'm not suggesting that you present your most intimate secrets to the general public, but it *is* important not to lie to yourself in your journal.

Bessel A. van der Kolk wrote in *The Body Keeps Score: Brain, Mind, and Body in the Healing of Trauma*, "As long as you keep secrets and suppress information, you are fundamentally at war with yourself."[24] I remember a time in my life when a romantic partner revealed a secret he had kept for almost two years. In the weeks that followed, I felt like I had increased my IQ. Everything made sense. All the confused pieces of my life formed a coherent puzzle. I had not realized how hard I worked trying not to know the secret that permeated our lives. George Orwell wrote in *1984*, "If you want to keep a secret, you must also hide it from yourself."[25] The trouble is our minds and bodies won't be fooled, and, as Shakespeare wrote, "Truth will out."[26] What truths are you trying not to know?

◆◆◆

Lies and secrets can weigh you down if they are not shared, faced, and dealt with. The nonjudgmental page of a journal is the perfect place to start revealing and addressing anything that you fear or anything you've kept hidden for too long. Living with negative memories feels like building up a corrosive layer around the soul. Keeping traumatic memories to oneself or fearing to reveal that one has been a victim also contributes to a feeling of being alienated. In other words, it contributes to a sense that there must be something wrong with you in order for that incident to have happened to you.

Likewise, if you don't reveal your stories or release your traumatic memories in a healthy way, such as through professional counseling, the fact that others have gone through such experiences, too, and have gone on to recover and live productive and happy lives might not be revealed to you. You might not have that perspective as a source of strength as you face obstacles in your journey to wholeness. Consider these statistics and know that whatever circumstance you might have faced alone and still carry with you, others have faced as well:

- RAINN (Rape, Abuse, & Incest National Network) estimate that a person is sexually assaulted every 73 seconds, and every nine minutes, that victim is a child.[27]
- According to the 2018 U.S. Census, about 17% of all American children were living in poverty.[28]
- *The Washington Post* shared a survey in which 54% of women reported facing sexual harassment at work, although about 90% of those said they never filed formal complaints for fear of embarrassment or professional retaliation.[29]

- According to *PewTrust.org*, in the United States, more than five million children, or one in 14, have had a parent in the state or federal prison system.[30]
- *Child Trends* reported that in 2014, 64% of children ages 14 to 17 say they were a witness to violence in their lifetimes.[31]
- The 1996 National Household Survey on Drug Abuse (NHSDA) reported that more than eight million children or 11% of all children in the USA live in homes in which at least one parent is an alcoholic or in need of other substance abuse treatment.[32]
- *The Washington Post* summarized various polls that show between 25% and 72% of all married people have cheated on their spouse.[33]

These statistics, of course, represent just some types of trauma that one might carry around as a negative secret, a burden they have not shared. I included these statistics not to stir up your bad feelings from the past or to make you sad, but to help readers understand no matter what trauma you have held in, there are professionals with experience to help you as you explore and resolve issues you might once have been encouraged to keep as a secret. As Lucille Clifton said, "Every pair of eyes facing you has seen something you would not have endured."[34] You are not alone.

Journaling about how such incidents might have affected your present life is often a good first step to claiming your resilience in conjunction with guidance from an experienced mental health professional. The point of journaling is not to stumble around in the past forever, but to locate the ways previous trauma might still be affecting us in order to choose new patterns of behavior which work better for us. Ann Aguirre wrote that "Once exposed, a secret loses all its power."[35] If your background were dissected by historians or a political opponent, what would come to light? How would it change your story? How would it change the fiction you believe others hold of you? What have your eyes seen that weaker souls could not have survived? When will be an appropriate time to reveal the events that made you who you are today? Is it possible that sharing your secret could strengthen others with similar experiences?

As you explore unpleasant aspects of your past circumstances, you may wish to establish rituals for emotional protection. Selecting an appropriate crystal to keep in one hand as you write with the other or to set on your desk as you journal about scary topics, can provide not only guardian energy but also remind you of your present safety. The choosing, holding, or viewing of a natural stone combines physical action to your mental thoughts, and symbolically, when you set down the crystal, you can set down the memory, trauma, or disturbance. I find black tourmaline useful when delving into previous trauma because this black stone is known not only for its superior protective energy, but for its ability to root one to the here and now. Expelling negativity, whether its source is outside of you in the form of a person or situation or coming from within your thoughts in the form of a memory of a past incident, holding the tourmaline stone may increase your own sense of power. As a traditional stone meant to bridge the physical to the spiritual, it makes excellent rosary beads. Black tourmaline also promotes healing and reduces stress, which can aid the therapeutic exploration of past experiences.

♦ ♦ ♦

At this point, I must address any teachers who might be using journaling with students. When Jana J. Turbyfill and Richard Fulkerson introduced me to journal writing in a classroom setting, I quickly learned that I could not make a promise to keep what underage students wrote in their notebooks completely confidential. Teachers today, no doubt, know that they are mandated reporters and have no choice but to share with Child Protective Services any suspicion that a child might have been abused or neglected.

As I read students' writing, I come to know them better and can form lessons better suited to their interests and needs, but certainly, to reap the emotional benefits of journaling, students must trust that their writing will be kept confidential. We teachers have no reason to share information about a student's crush on the kid in his art class or about a child being sleepy because her parents' argument about the father's unemployment had kept her awake all night. I quickly learned that I needed to explain to students what I am required by law or my personal ethical standards to reveal, including, of course, plans to commit a crime, the committing of a past crime, any type of abuse or neglect, or other illegal or harmful behaviors. "It doesn't mean you can't write about those things or that I don't want to know if this is happening to you so I can get you some help," I now explain, "but I am a legally mandated reporter, so if something bad is happening to you, I have to report it. It can't stay a secret for your journal, you, and me."

I also give teenagers the opportunity to turn in journals with pages folded in half and stapled, glued, taped, or clipped and marked "Confidential. Do not read." Believe it or not, even when they consciously know I read their entries, students begin to write for themselves and for their own reasons when journals are graded only for completion, not for content or mechanics. Likewise, if our journals are read or shared by those to whom we have not given permission, either to serve someone else's agenda or satisfy a wondering mind, it can take a long time to re-establish the sanctity of our journals.

◆ ◆ ◆

Of course, trauma isn't the only kind of secret we might be keeping. Some of our secrets are probably humorous, or we might have memories of sensing that something was amiss as children, before the secret (a parent's upcoming divorce, bad blood between your father and his sister, bankruptcy, etc.) was revealed to us as adults. As Jean Ferris wrote in *Once Upon a Marigold*, "Secrets have a way of making themselves felt, even before you know there's a secret."[36] If this resonates with you, write a journal entry about a secret that was kept from you. Write about how you interpreted bits of whispered conversation about a secret or how you felt when a secret from the past was revealed to you at last. As a child once asked me when the secret of her father's identity was finally revealed to her by her mother, "Why didn't she just tell me?" I agree with that sentiment about most secrets, and in general, I think trying to keep even the unsavory details of one's own story hidden tends to do more harm than good for all involved. Our minds are prone to create stories and make up our own answers to questions unless we are presented with the full truth, and too often for children the answers are: I must have done something wrong or there must be something wrong with me.

As you consider this topic, ask yourself, what were the reasons a secret was kept from you? Did those hiding something from you have your best interest at heart? Was their plan ultimately effective or destructive for you? Are you holding onto any secrets that might have major effects on those around you?

Certainly, it is rare for people *not* to have a few skeletons in their closets. When the welcoming attitude and newly embraced transparency of a local Catholic Church won me over, I was charged with making my first confession, and I joked that I might need to find younger priests. The middle-agers in my parish, I explained, might not live long enough to hear my full confession. But, in all seriousness, I also felt how freeing it was to finally be released from the power of those secret sins—some of them silly, like sneaking out a ream of blue art paper in middle school forty years ago and some of them serious, like actions and decisions that truly hurt people I loved. I believe in acknowledging the ways in which we have disappointed ourselves or hurt our fellowmen, but I also believe my friend Mary Belcher's mantra. "Guilt," she said to me as I underwent the painful process of adolescence in East Texas, "is excess baggage." What skeletons have been rattling for you long enough? Let them come out to play on the pages of your journal.

◆◆◆

I tend to be a quiet flier. If seatmates open a book or pop in their earphones, they needn't be worried I will chatter to them throughout the flight. My grandmother came West in a covered wagon, and just knowing that within two generations, I could be eating warm shrimp pasta with a cold glass of white wine thousands of feet in the sky is a technological leap I could silently meditate on forever. However, I've often been amazed when my neighbors on an airplane have not only been talkative but have shared with me their most precious stories or fabulous secrets. I've met a woman who once wanted to be a nun but now had six children. I've met an elderly woman who worked on airplane wings during World War II and missed the job when she was relegated back to the roles of wife and mother. I've met many newly divorced or recently widowed travelers wondering aloud what the future holds for them.

There is something about the buzz of an airplane's engine, the engineering miracle of flight, and the anonymity of a stranger that allows us to share things we might not have revealed to our best friends or even to ourselves. In *Harvey*, Elwood P. Dowd, my role model in life, explains that his companions at the local pub come in and tell him (and his invisible, six-foot-tall rabbit) about their lives, their troubles, their hopes, and dreams because, as he says, "no one ever brings anything small into a bar."[37] Whether you have the experience of confiding in a stranger on an airplane, a local bartender, a trusted best friend, or a paid counselor, think of your journal as another place to share those big, real things that constitute your life.

◆ ◆ ◆

My students and participants in my writing workshops sometimes express a fear of someone finding and reading their journal. I have to admit that I keep a "fit to be photocopied and distributed" journal at my workplace and a "no holds barred" journal at home for just this reason. I find though that as I grow more mature and as I have taken more responsibility for my own life and decisions, I don't have the need to hide my thoughts from others quite so much.

One woman told me she would never write because her husband might read what she wrote. If what she wrote would send him into a violent rage or would reveal that she never loved him as she had his cousin Bubba, the journaling process might be leading her to a decision to escape that marriage anyway. But, if she were just processing her dissatisfaction with, say, the distribution of work around the house or if she were just venting about some habit that annoyed her, my feeling is: if what he reads hurts his feelings, that is his fault for invading her privacy, not her fault for writing her feelings down. Your journal is your private space. Set that expectation. My grandchildren who sometimes share my home know not to read my journal, nor do I read theirs. Likewise, my partner knows my journal is off limits, although I often share with him much of what I have written.

Once though, I dated a man who had three teenage children. The kids were still struggling to come to terms with their parents' divorce and much of their angst and confusion was directed at me, although I'd not met the man until after his marriage ended. In my journal, as I was attempting to get to know them, I wrote about each child and what I thought they were going through. I wrote about where we were in our relationship, about what I loved about them, what their strengths were, and about how their approval or disapproval felt to me. The journal I kept on my bedroom nightstand, and after one visit I noticed a page had disappeared from my notebook. Obviously, one of the children had looked through the journal and taken it.

Despite the invasion of privacy, I was actually glad they had seen the journal. Tensions among us were so great I would never have felt comfortable approaching the subjects I'd written about with those sweet young adults, and I was glad that my written words had found their way to that audience for which they were not penned. Truth had surfaced at a time when they, their parents, and I were all wrestling to know what was truth and what had the ring of a lie.

My point is if you have issues keeping your journal private, there are probably other issues with which you need to be dealing. Are you setting appropriate boundaries for yourself and others? Are you in an untrusting relationship? Is your living situation safe? Are you somehow being intimidated from thinking critically or expressing yourself authentically? Are you, in fact, engaging in behavior that would harm others should it surface as all truth does, indeed, sooner or later?

If you are in a healthy situation, you will be able to tell those who have access to your home that your journal is private, that you spin out your problems, vent, and say things in the journal you wouldn't necessarily say out loud. If you have children, establish a journal-writing culture in your home early. In a favorite snapshot with my granddaughter, we're both sitting beside each other with our journals. At two years old, she appears for all the world to be writing in her book as feverishly as I am writing in mine. Likewise, my grandson has a journal, although he's only in kindergarten. Each day we form a couple of sentences together, and he traces the words and draws a picture to accompany them. The location of his journal is very important to him!

I tend to keep a journal in my purse and work satchel. It's always handy that way, and there is no doubt that it is my personal property. Just as no one but a thief would pull out my lipsticks and use them, no one in my daily life would pull out my journal and read my musings without explicit permission.

◆◆◆

Of course, not all secrets are negative ones. As I've grown older, I've become less shy about saying what I think. I believe this is due in large part to reading my old journals as I happen across them in a cedar chest or at the bottom of a moving box. My journal has taught me that the uncensored me in my head is clever and funny, passionate and poetic, and knowledgeable about many issues. I guarantee that if you write long enough, your journal will teach you these same lessons about yourself.

Your journals will also reveal some weak points. Do you have a pattern of ignoring big red flags? Did you bury your instincts and pay the price? Do you habitually complain about the same thing without taking any action to make a change? What phrases come up again and again in your writing? What do they tell you about how you are living your life, whether or not you are enjoying your days or your work or your relationships? What phrases would you like to see more often in your journal, and ultimately, in your life?

Remember the old joke, I wouldn't want to be a member of any club that would have me as a member? Often, we are much harder on and more critical of ourselves than we would be on any other rational adult. The truth is, most people don't mind our being a bit flawed or even being a lot less than perfect. Perfect people are sometimes hard to be around! When you use journaling to focus on or even to reveal to yourself positive traits you have, you will find yourself opening up more to people, and in that open space friendships blossom. In fact, the flawed, secret you could be the you who attracts great people and amazing situations into your life.

◆ ◆ ◆

As a child, did you have a secret hiding place where you kept your "treasures"? If so, what did you list among those prized items? Why were they special or worth keeping? I love the opening to the film version of *To Kill a Mockingbird* in which Scout's hands are seen examining a broken watch, the two dolls we learn were made by Boo Radley, and a few other items the children held dear.[38] What items are you holding in a secret place?

Do you also hide your talents or your secret wishes and craziest fantasies? I, for example, have wanted to play Blanche DuBois in a community production of *A Streetcar Named Desire* for as long as I can remember.[39] However, I am getting long in the tooth for such a role and have no real acting experience unless you count Sunday school plays or having once taken part in *The Vagina Monologues* as presented at the Flying Monkey Arts Center in Huntsville, Alabama.[40] Your journal is a place to admit that you'd like to do something crazy!

I'll always be thankful for Julia Cameron's idea of "artist's dates" for giving me permission to visit an unusual church. For months, I had followed the progress of an old bus that set up camp along an Alabama highway I traveled almost daily. One day its disheveled owner painted "Mission Jesus Saves" on the side, and soon other characters started arriving. Finally, I mustered up the courage to attend a "singing," telling myself it was an "artist date." In addition to sitting on lawn chairs and enjoying old songs from my youth in a rural Baptist church, I finally got to meet and hear the bus owner. He was accompanied by a beautiful young woman with a baby who appeared to have also taken up residence at the camp and an array of other people upon whose likenesses I could establish an endless series of southern gothic novels.

During the sermon, the old man preached about how we are called to "witness to" sinners where they are. His words inadvertently revealed that his favorite place to "witness" was in a bar with cheap beer, but somehow this made him no less holy to the crowd. And, frankly, in his honesty, he seemed well-intentioned and harmless to me as well. It was an experience I have savored for years and about which I have written novel chapters and poems.

That night and all the writing and sharing that came thereafter were a direct result of having a journal that demanded I call attention to my thoughts and my surroundings. If I had not sat down and admitted on the page my fascination with the "Mission Jesus Saves" bus, I would not have encountered those beautiful people, their words and voices, and the juxtaposed sanctity and inadvertent humor of the evening. That would be a shame because what started as permission from Cameron to, "go to a crazy church service" became a lesson in the charming, faulty ways of man in search of truth. Journaling will lead you to new places! Enjoy the ride!

◆ ◆ ◆

What did you want to be when you grew up? Our fantasy lives are often much more interesting than the lives we present to the world. Think of "The Secret Life of Walter Mitty" in which Mitty's fantasies of himself entertain readers of James Thurber's story much more than Mitty's conventional real life.[41] Likewise, the true secrets revealed between friends can deepen a friendship. I think of co-workers who became friends during our travels together around the country because of what they revealed to me about their pasts, their secret desires, and their habits. These secrets let me know of their heartaches and deferred dreams, the events that had shaped them, flattened them, or made them stronger.

When I was a student in Bogata Junior High School, we played a fortune-telling game. We would make a list of four people we might marry, and the number of children we might have—these first two things being of utmost importance in a church where one sometimes went immediately from the youth group to the young-married Sunday school class. We also listed cities or towns in which we wanted to live, the job we wanted to have, and the car we wanted to drive. We'd then pick a number and count through the list crossing out the item landed on when we reached our chosen number. Finally, there would be only one item left in each category.

As I sit in the big middle of a life which I have created in no small part by journaling, I often think of that game and of how many times I rigged the number to land me in Dallas, the city in which I now live, and in Paris, France, a city I have been fortunate to visit at least once a year for the past seven years. Writing about my dreams has helped me make them realities, and we'll talk more about that later. But now, I mention my annual sojourn to Paris because while Paris has many things to offer—croissants that melt in your mouth, cheese that will make you swear the pasteurized grocery store versions you buy at home are plastic facsimiles of real food, the waft of French perfume as a chic woman passes you— the reason I return to Paris year after year is because it gifts me with its almost palpable approval of journal keepers.

Annually, I go to Paris to attend a writing workshop called Paris Café Writing led by Patricia Tennison, but I travel alone. That trip represents the two weeks I breathe most deeply, walk most freely, and bask both in the abiding friendships developed over the years with my writing group and in my solitude. The other fifty weeks of the year, however, I use my journal as a kind of escape. A journal represents another way of being truly alone with yourself. It's the ultimate me time. During COVID-19, the tragic, criminal, and unnecessary death of George Floyd, and all the other strangeness that attended 2020, my journal allowed me to climb into its blank pages and rest. I was able to set down my wild thoughts, sometimes acknowledging and sometimes pushing aside my fears, and always expressing my political opinions in a quiet, non-judgmental space without fearing the wrath of friends whose opinions might run contrary to mine. What I want to share with the world, I can and do through several social media venues, but that which finds its way into my journal includes what I want to keep to myself or write in an effort to explore all sides of issues in an attempt to build empathy. These things I happily do in, you guessed it, secret.

If you have the opportunity to go to a foreign country alone for two weeks a year, what will you do there? Where will you stay? If you could slow down and take a stroll through a beautiful French park, what might you think about? Explore your travel fantasies in your journal; it's the first step in making those secret dreams come true.

Explore, too, your secret version of the fortune that might have been created for you had you played the game I played as a youth. What cities or towns would you want to live in or visit if family and work weren't holding you to any particular location? What other jobs might you like to try? When you are in a car and your mind wanders, what daydreams do you entertain? Walter Mitty's daydreams were far from the life he felt bound to in Thurber's short story. What Walty Mitty fantasies do you have? Explore them. Writing is a form of honoring and acknowledging. Once you have done this, you'll find opportunities to transform these daydreams into realities. As my friend, Colet Williams, who hosts the podcast *Eat the Damn Bread*, would say, "Your dreams are not pie in the sky! You can do this!"

In 1987, during my first year of teaching, my students and I wrote our own versions of Thurber's work. I wrote about singing a beautiful aria. In 2012, I gave a small dinner party that I still think of as one of my highlights as a hostess, because it was one of those gatherings when just the right people came together in just the right mood. Eventually, guests pulled out harmonicas and guitars, recited poems, and sang songs. Before the night was over, my friend Iris Petra Jacobs and I belted out, "Nessun Dorma." My fantasy life blended into my real life in spite of my not being able to carry a tune and not knowing Italian. I smile thinking of Iris' beautiful voice, competing with my range of off-key notes. Those moments are among my favorite memories, not because of our stellar performance, but because I was living my secret dream.

In my journal, I have often begun new phases of my life, new career steps, new college degrees, new relationships, and new homes. The safety a journal provides has become a transitional step between my dreams' being a secret and my dreams' coming true. Trust that your journal welcomes thoughts that begin as, "Maybe, after all, I really could . . . ."

The secrecy provided within a journal can also give you the space you need to consider your feelings about your present situation. A few years ago my life became extremely busy with family obligations, a fulltime job, travel, and writing whenever I could grab time to do so. Suddenly, my friends, who had once been able to call up and say, "Free this afternoon?" were finding that I had to carefully carve out time for evenings out or quick lunches. As my time became more limited, I became choosy about how I spent my free hours. I began recording in my journal how I felt as I made plans with friends. Was I excited to get a call or invitation, or did I dread receiving a text asking me to get together? When I left the person, did I feel inspired, accepted, heard, or valued? Did I have fun and laugh? Did we discuss problems or catch up on each other's lives?

Taking this close look on paper led me to make more deliberate decisions about how I wanted to spend my time. After writing about outings with one friend, I found that when we went out alone, I loved our conversations and activities, but when we went out as part of a group, the conversations seemed stilted, dull, and superficial. Noting this in my journal entries, I was able to plan more one-on-one time and less group time with this friend.

Likewise, I spotted one friendship into which I wanted to put less energy. Each time my friend invited me somewhere, I felt guilty if I said no. Inevitably, if I had a conflict, my "not this time" was met with "It's been so long since we've seen each other. I've been going through some bad times." After we spent time together, I started noting in my journal that I'd felt compelled to stay longer than I wanted to, that I'd felt it necessary to pick up the check yet again, and that I'd felt trapped during our time and depleted when I left. As a non-judgmental listener, I'd become an enabler for his depressive state, rather than a helper.

During one of our last private times together when he was explaining, yet again, how he'd been going through some rough times and how this event or that event had been depressing to him, I finally said, "You know, I've known you for about eight years now, and every time we get together, I feel like you have been experiencing some crisis. I wonder what we can do so that when these things occur they don't bring you down so much? Can we make a plan so that you can anticipate some of these normal, everyday downers and be ready when they occur?" It turns out, he didn't want to do that. He leapt into the next bad thing— a date that had gone wrong or what had happened at the event that I missed even though he "was so looking forward to seeing [me] there but [I] couldn't go." I still loved my friend, but I made a mental note that I was going to see him mostly at social gatherings and group events. Such settings seemed somehow to dissipate his negative energy and enliven him, and I always enjoyed the dinner parties or gala receptions we had attended together. There's a fine line between a friend in need and an emotional vampire. Journaling about how you feel before and after a planned visit with a friend can help you make the distinction.

As a single woman, I had once followed advice to make a list of all the qualities I was looking for in a partner. A journal is a good place for that kind of exercise, and the same process can work with friends. As an adolescent you might have thought or even written, "I wish I could be friends with . . . ." As an adult, it is worth pursuing such thinking again. What qualities do you want your friends to have? How do you want to feel before, during, and after an interaction with your friends? These aren't just the social anxiety questions that bedevil middle school children. These are important questions for grown-up and growing adults. Jim Rohn, author of *Leading an Inspired Life*, once said that we are the average of the five people with whom we spend the most time.[42] Who are those people in your life? Are they bringing to the table the ingredients you want to form your ideal self? If not, who do you know or want to meet and befriend who has these qualities? What traits do you want to emulate? Who do you know who has mastered these traits? In other words, what do you secretly think about the people you are spending time with, and with whom do you *want* to be friends?

One of my favorite things to do is compare the inside and outside of myself. Using Carol Tuttle's "Dressing Your Truth" system,[43] I've begun to align the way I look on the outside with the ways I navigate the world according to my personality type. Still, all of us have the self we show to the world and the secret self we are inside. Recently, I spoke with an old classmate of mine. She explained that we had different experiences in school. She hated every minute of it, while I enjoyed my high school years.

During our conversation, she revealed that she felt different because her family was poor. I believe she assumed that I knew this. In fact, I was oblivious to any difference in our parents' finances, but her perception of herself as poor had clouded our relationship. My assumption when we began to grow apart was that she preferred cooler kids, and I was just studious and square. I wish I had checked my perceptions and hers; we could have been better friends all through those years and probably into our adulthood.

In your journal, create two collages or write two entries. For one, write or create an image of how you believe you are perceived on the outside. For the other, write or create an image of how you feel you are on the inside. Consider those elements that you secretly believe define you now or defined you in the past. How do your perceptions surrounding social position or financial circumstances taint a view of yourself as worthy of success?

◆ ◆ ◆

Journals can be used to record dreams, dreams which reveal the most hidden parts of our pasts, present realities, or even future possibilities. It's no wonder we humans are fascinated by dreams and that in them, rest many of our secrets and our deepest truths. Our subconscious mind pulls up images that can be interpreted as symbols, which allows us to visit people in our past and examine those relationships anew. Journals, if approached thoughtfully, can become the vehicle for revealing subconscious truths to ourselves. Great literary works are full of accounts of dreams that contained messages from angels or from a higher power. In fact, it was in a dream that God told Joseph to take Mary and Jesus and get out of Dodge, so to speak, and then in a dream God gave Joseph the all clear to return from Egypt after Herod died. While our dreams might not contain such clear and divine messages, the assemblage of images, characters, actions, and statements rolling around in our subconscious often contain meaning if we look closely enough. We sometimes ignore our intuition consciously, but remembered dreams knock on the door of our conscious mind and demand entrance.

I write down my dreams not because I believe they are prophecies or angel-inscribed messages but doing so has taught me to trust my intuition more. I once dreamed of being bitten by a snake and the next day was fired from a job I really needed at the time. By reading old journals, I noticed warning signs I had missed. The job was a secretarial position requiring an eye for detail I simply do not have. On the other hand, while working in a curriculum-writing job I loved and had not thought about leaving, I once dreamed of another position as an on-campus instructional coach for teachers. In the dream, I loved the job and found it fully satisfying. I woke up the next morning to the phone ringing. When my friend on the other line offered me a job as a coach for teachers at the school where she had just accepted an administrative position, I suddenly knew what it meant when people said, "The hair on the back of my neck stood up." Had I not had that dream, I might have turned down the job that led me to a new sense of awareness and humility I would often rely on in my future.

In your journal, explore the most secret part of your knowledge base, and the worlds created by your dreaming self. What longings surface in your dreams? Have you ever received messages in your dreams that served you well in life? As you record your dreams in your journal, you might spot patterns or themes. What are they? If there is a lesson in your most recent dream, what is it? What objects reoccur in your dreams, and what might they symbolize? Dreams have been a part of your awareness as long as you have been on Earth. What attitudes and beliefs have you held about dreams? From where did those presumptions originate? If you believe you don't remember your dreams, write a journal in which you pretend your dream catcher worked. What might be caught and revealed? Allow yourself to play, to be frightened, to acknowledge the symbols trapped in the web of your dream catcher, struggling to be acknowledged.

◆ ◆ ◆

Your journal will act as a safety net, allowing you to come to terms with societal realities versus societal ideals, and release the thought that "if people knew" most of your secrets, you would be alone and friendless. Most people think about us much less than we think they do, and most people worth knowing well are accepting of our flaws, mistakes, and yes, even our deepest secrets. Journaling can teach you to forgo self-rapprochement and shame and explore the questions: What or who do I need to evict from my mind? What would I do if there were no judgment from other people? What would I do if I knew I would not fail?

I agree with Rainer Maria Rilke in that "I want to be with those who know secret things or else alone" in life and in literature.[44] In *The Great Gatsby*, Fitzgerald lures us into the mystery surrounding the book's namesake by introducing us to a narrator whose first confession is that he is often told things he'd rather not have known, "the secret griefs of wild, unknown men," thereby ensuring readers a tale worth hearing.[45] I own journals full of secrets, including accounts of despair and abuse, wild fantasies and crazy wishes, scraps of gossip and slices of wisdom, and theories about mysteries. To my journal, I tell all my innermost secrets, even those I'm not quite ready to tell anyone else. I verbalize on paper the me I shroud from public view, and I practice opening the curtains of the stage on which I am "merely [a] player."[46] Elvis Presley once said, "Truth is like the sun. You can shut it out for a time, but it ain't goin' away." Journals are constantly ready to receive your truth whether it comes wrapped in sadness, timidness, or hope.

Chapter 5: Reflective You

"Self-reflection is the school of wisdom."

—Baltasar Gracián[48]

Journals are a source of instant replay for savoring or for dissecting experiences as a way of rehearsing better options for future behavior, decisions, and responses. Journals are the antidote for an unexamined life. Recording your thoughts forces you to generate clear ideas and to engage metacognitively in the messages entertained by your brain, granting you more control and more choice over what you will think, say, and do in the future.

For example, in my journal I eradicated a barrier to success I had never acknowledged but by which I was obstructed for almost forty years. When I started working on my Ph.D., I wrote these words in my journal: "I wonder if I need a doctorate to do the work I'm really doing?" in writing down those words, I realized their source—a middle school math teacher tasked with recording the career and education goals of graduating 8th graders. "What kind of job do you want?" she droned, clipboard in hand. "I want to be a travel writer." She smirked.

"And, if that doesn't happen?" I was a good little writer and our junior high Valedictorian, and every Wednesday night I went to a mission study class at church in which I'd learned about foreign countries through a magazine produced by the church organization. I'd also read *National Geographic* in the Bogata Elementary School library, so I knew such jobs existed both in the religious and secular worlds. Still, the teacher sat there waiting for another, less comical answer.

"I would love to be a teacher," I said and meant it. She wrote that down. It was an acceptable answer in Red River County in the late 1970s. When she asked, "What kind of education do you think you'll get?" I didn't hesitate to answer, "I want a Ph.D." At that, the teacher could no longer contain herself and actually laughed out loud. When she composed herself, she asked, "Do you think you'll need a Ph.D. for the kind of job you're *really* going to have?" I shrugged and answered with embarrassment, "I don't know. I just want one."

Before I wrote in my journal and acknowledged this conversation, I had started three other Ph.D. programs, but I always seemed to ask myself, "Do I need a Ph.D. for the kind of job I'm *really* going to have?" which made me stop the effort before I ever got started. Obviously, I did grow up to be a writer. I've also led dozens of high school students to Europe, and I run a small company, allowing me to guide adult writers to foreign locations for writing retreats. Equally important, I am a teacher. When I finally wrote down and explored my old teacher's question in my journal, I realized I was writing English curricula for all the high school teachers in one of the ten largest urban districts in the United States. I had been the Chair of the National Board Certified English Teachers Assembly. I had published in the most well-known scholarly journal for my profession. Ultimately, I wrote in my journal, "Yes, ma'am, it turns out I *do* need a Ph.D. for the job I really have."

This one notwithstanding, I have been blessed with countless wonderful and supportive instructors from first grade through my current graduate work. Sadly, students everywhere sometimes face their own versions of that middle school teacher, a person who discourages any dream extending beyond the local neighborhood. Once upon a time in a rural land far away, I sat across the desk from a teacher on a sticky Texas day, and it took almost forty years and a fresh journal page to banish her and reinvent myself as a person doing meaningful work, deserving of as much education as I wanted to receive. Reflecting in a journal allowed me to write, "Get out of my head, lady! The Universe has great plans for my life that neither you nor I could have imagined!"

A journal can take your past on a playdate. It can let you explore your own life at a distance. It can also act as a tool for deconstructing your past, while savoring memories and constructing a new future. The sheer act of writing helps journal keepers let go of pain, emancipating feelings through words and banishing the power of negative events and messages. Writing provides a second and sometimes richer experience of your own life. What voices from your past need to be re-examined? What messengers still have your ear? Reflect on your perception of yourself and what you deserve. If a voice or memory you don't like shows up, write about it until you have vacuumed up its power like spilled confetti thrown in celebration of an achievement someone once told you you'd never obtain. Don't let your limits be defined by someone who hasn't even seen the mountains on which you were destined to plant your flag!

The journal entry about which I spoke in the last section was a telescope, allowing me to see back to the past where I demanded a do over. Sometimes, however, journal writing can be more like a microscope, allowing you to view an experience or a conversation much more closely than you could in real time. It also allows you to simultaneously dissect it to view all its nuances and shades of hidden meaning.

After a typical day or an unusual or important experience, your journal practically rolls out a red carpet for your reflections. While the benefits of journaling far outweigh those of a log or a diary, considering how you spent the time you were given to live can lead to changes that amount to leaps that lead you closer to reaching your goals. What did you accomplish today? What will you remember? What pleased you or surprised you? What made this day different from any other? Your reflections move beyond merely recording your life events. Instead, journals allow you to reflect on the importance and meaning of the events.

Today, perhaps, you spent two hours in a department store, browsing home goods you don't really need. The journaling shopper asks, "Why?" Are you unsatisfied with your home or a relationship? Is there something you are trying to distract yourself from? Is it truly that you wanted a pop of color in the form of a new throw pillow, or has shopping become a pastime or a habit? Were you motivated by the thrill of purchasing something new? How does your home stack up to the ideal home in your fantasies?

Without a doubt, some elements of life must be seen through—the course you detest that is part of a degree plan, a painful visit to the dentist, even the loss of a loved one. While working for the National Children's Advocacy Center, I remember a psychiatrist saying she was surprised that she went through all the stages of grief when her mother died. "I thought that because I knew about denial, anger, bargaining, depression, and acceptance, I'd be able to skip those components in real life. I wasn't, and I didn't." In these cases, journaling helps not only by giving us an expressive outlet for our feelings, frustrations, and even for our grief, but writing also helps us keep our eye on the big picture—a graduation, a nice smile, or the ability to remember our loved one with more appreciation than regret, anger, or sadness.

As I've mentioned previously, much of our life *is* within our control. Asking ourselves how and why a particular incident happened can help us avoid similar mistakes if mistakes have, indeed, been made. It can also let us release self-blame for incidents that might have made us feel bad, incidents which truly had little to do with us. What fears, for example, might have triggered the rage of a boss when we made a simple mistake or misunderstood directions? What would be the best way to make yourself heard in a meeting if someone keeps speaking over you? What might have been a better way to approach the waiter who failed to bring you the correct order at lunch and never offered a refill on your sweet tea? What conversations can we have tomorrow to take a step toward undoing damage we did today?

Reflecting allows us immediate gratification of letting go of our day. We can vent in our journal without getting a name as a complainer or a negative person. We can freeze an experience and work details out later when we are more emotionally prepared or when we simply have more time. We can rattle on about deeds irrelevant or educational, but we must examine ourselves through journaling to rise to a state of full consciousness and deliberate living. During his trial around 399 BC in Athens, Socrates famously declared, "An unexamined life is not worth living."[49] I agree it is our ability to reflect and to think critically that separates us from lesser species.

Fulfilling our human potential requires assessing our lives. We sometimes don't recognize the positive aspects of our lives. Did you make a stranger smile today by speaking as you passed? Did you respond with harshness when it would have been just as easy to have been kind? I think, for instance, of the homeless man standing in the road clapping a song when on impulse, I set down a salad I'd saved from lunch near his things for him to find later. Suddenly, he turned around and said with sincerity, "You are a token of beauty." Then, he returned to his song.

There is a theory that we only do things for others because of the way it makes us feel about ourselves. Perhaps this is true, which is not good news for most of us since we are told that "the humble are granted grace."[50] The results are the same: people are affected positively. What did you fail to do today, and in contrast what was your biggest accomplishment or your most significant act of service? Did you do all you could with a spirit of love to others, or were you too trapped in your own head to pay attention to those placed around you? Examine your life but do it not just in terms of how you have been affected by whatever your day brought you, but also by what you have contributed to the lives of others. As John Dewey said, "We do not learn from experience, we learn from reflecting on experience."[51]

♦♦♦

A goal of this book is to lead you down the path to your ideal life, the one you dream about, but selecting this book lets me know you are not where you want to be in every area of your life . . . well, not yet anyway! One of the ways we sabotage our own happiness is by blinding ourselves with nostalgia. The reality is that the good ol' days were no better or worse than the days we experience in contemporary times. We don our poodle skirts, go to a sock-hop themed party, and talk about "more innocent" times. In actuality, disenchantment and loss, discontent and struggle, immorality and the plagues of racism and injustice were just as much a part of our collective psyches then as they are now, and the same could be said of any time period.

Having taught in high schools for half of my life, I am perpetually disturbed by those who tell young people that these are the best days of their lives. Do those grownups not remember the stress of a difficult course, an unrequited love, a school bully, a catty school chum's scathing comments whispered just loudly enough that you could hear, the constant struggle between the parent who wants to hold onto their child and the teenager who longed for more independence and freedom? Have they blotted out the pressure to fit in, to be considered one of the in-crowd? Every age comes with its own challenges and its own joys, and they all deserve to be preserved on the pages of your journal. Such writing provides a guard against nostalgia and a reminder that we have made it through tough times before and can again. Beyond being a tool for documenting what you did on a particular day, the journal as a historical document or pseudo-autobiography, helps you remember who you were and use that point as a springboard to becoming a better, happier, more successful version of *you*. Whether you're reviewing a journal from thirty years ago or thirty minutes ago, journals remind you of who you once were.

Even if you're just beginning a journal, you can still benefit through your current pages. Write, for example, about something you once believed that you no longer believe. Write about something—a possession, a relationship, a job— you believed you wanted but somehow wasn't satisfying in the way you thought it would be. Take your time and write about your best and worst memories at every age. What were you warned away from as a child? In what ways do the things that gave you pleasure as a child still thrill you? If you wish, for example, take a look at "Personal Helicon," a poem by Irish writer, Seamus Heaney, in which he describes a penchant for exploring wells and hearing his echo in the darkness, something he then likens to authoring poetry.[52]

Conversely, how have you disconnected from the silly, fun things that gave you joy as a child? Did you like to skate or play the piano? Did you draw or color or paint? Did you ride a bike, pick flowers and press them in the pages of books, or fence using wooden rulers instead of swords? What fun are you denying yourself because it isn't dignified for someone of your oh-so-grown-up stature? Journals can become guidebooks, leading us forward to wonderful lives but also allowing us to borrow and replicate the joys of the past as well.

In an episode of the old television series, *The Wonder Years,* Kevin shows us that when we are children, we are allowed to be a little bit artist, musician, scholar, and athlete.[53] As we grow older, being mature demands a process of giving up those things at which we do not clearly excel even if we enjoy them. What have you given up that you would like to reclaim? In what ways is the process satisfying enough to justify results that aren't perfect?

◆ ◆ ◆

Journals don't just record how you spend your time; they record what you were doing in a period of time. In other words, journals allow you to bear witness to history. Think about the historic events that have occurred during your lifetime. Depending on your age, you might have been alive when atomic bombs were dropped on Japan, when the Little Rock Nine bravely integrated Arkansas schools, or when the Twin Towers fell in New York. Answering the question, "Where were you when . . . ?" can leave a valuable historic record.

As I write this book, we Americans are living through the old curse, "May you live in interesting times." Writers' astute awareness of historic events can infiltrate the pages of their notebooks, and—should you choose not to demand your journals' destruction upon your death—will delight future generations of readers, who spot your thoughts about some character or event about which they have only read in history books among the irrelevant, foolish, and sublime meandering immortalized by your journal. Journals record memories. The cranky poet Charles Bukowski once said, "Some moments are nice, some are nicer, some are even worth writing about."[54] I would argue that many moments, especially moments of extreme human strife or joy or drama, are always worth writing about. You and your life are always worth the expulsion of ink onto paper. Historical events, significant political shifts, a global pandemic and how it has affected you and your daily routines—all are worth mentioning in your writing. Embrace your role as a witness to history.

As you reflect on your days, don't forget to note simple delights, such as overheard snippets of conversation that please you or ironic scenes that grab hold of your imagination. I think of a young man, wearing a long cowboy-style duster, crossing a highway against an Alabama hill with the sun setting in the background through tree leaves of cinnabar and vermilion, making him a walking silhouette. I think of a beautiful young woman I passed on another highway my first year of teaching. She was hitchhiking, I suppose, and had stopped to look at a pasture in East Texas. She looked for all the world like she'd just come from Woodstock, and her face had the most contented countenance I have ever seen on a human being. I think of the lonely high schooler walking toward a local auditorium with his graduation robes over his shoulder. I think of a teenage girl, at least six months pregnant, joyfully riding a skateboard in the parking lot near a housing project. I've devoted journal pages to their memories and to wondering about the stories that led them to the moment I spotted them, living their lives. Journaling allows us to capture the characters that dance in and out of our worlds in a flash, becoming snapshots in our memory, those who we might not fully appreciate or those who go on to become inhabitants in the poems or fiction we write. Our journals then become idea incubators, helping us nurture and grow new stories.

I think of conversations I've had and recorded in my journal that might otherwise have long been forgotten. I think of the older man left to sit on a bench at a bookstore while his daughter prowled around and how we struck up a conversation about how he couldn't sleep through a whole night since he survived Hurricane Katrina in New Orleans. He told me about his terrors and the images that haunted him. I think of conversations I have overheard. For example, in New Zealand I was having tea at a shop near an assisted living center when I spotted four of the residents dressed up and chatting over their tea. "Millie," said one, "I heard that Howard had asked you to marry him." Millie was at least ninety. "Yes," Millie said, "can you imagine? What did he want me to do at my age? Darn his socks?" The women giggled. "Well," said one mischievously, "as I remember I quite enjoyed darning socks." Her wit was so quick and her delivery so perfect, I nearly spit out my tea. Such scenes and conversations are gifts from the Universe, and writing them down is a way of saying, "Thank you!"

◆◆◆

Reflecting in our journal increases self-awareness, the foundation of social emotional intelligence. It helps us be more effective in all areas of our lives from personal to professional. It also provides opportunities to rehearse upcoming situations, and revisit situations that didn't go as well as we hoped, while reveling in situations about which we feel joyful or proud. A page written in your journal is one small daily accomplishment, something to show for even the worst or most unproductive of days. When we end the day, asking ourselves the question, "What did I accomplish?" we might be surprised by the answers and the patterns that show up, answers that might point to ways we are wasting time when we could have been helping someone, treating ourselves, or learning something new.

Relaxation, of course, is not the same as a waste of hours. Our bodies and minds work most efficiently when we are well-rested, and in times of stress, many of us need the solace of a nap, a lazy day, or an early bedtime. Reflection, though, can sound the alarm if we are spending too much time on social media or watching television or engaging in any activity that doesn't align with our goals or values. Reflection produces the ability to recognize patterns. Journal for more than two years, and you'll start noticing moods that match seasons or messages you tell yourself over and over. You will start discerning themes. You will start making discoveries about situations you repeat or that replicate a pattern picked up in your parents' home. Most importantly, you'll gain the ability to rewrite the story of *you*.

In America, we like to tell ourselves that "all men [and women] are created equal,"[55] but recent events have brought even the most privileged and the most oblivious of us to a point of recognition that we have a caste system in our country. Reflective journaling allows us to consider the ways in which we want to change that system to benefit all Americans. It also allows us a place to be real about the class, background, and communities from which we come. It allows us to take inventory of the ways our society has shaped us and determine the extent we wish to change traditionally told stories. It allows us to examine the stories society tells about ethnicity, race, religion, sexual orientation, gender, and age. Reflection allows us to consciously decide what parts of these stories we want to accept and what parts we want to reject and rewrite!

If your story has been that you will only go so far in life or that you will only rise to a particular level in your field and rise no more, a journal is the place in which you can start revising that story. Train yourself to walk what Joseph Campbell identified as the "hero's journey" on which you are called to an adventure, face obstacles, confront foes, learn lessons, and bring home the boons you set out to obtain.[56] You don't have to conform to the plot of a story in which you don't end up a heroic figure in a place that feeds your soul. Change your story. Use your journal to write an ongoing life story that suits you, one with a setting and characters and plot points that please you!

Reflection allows us to brainstorm solutions to problems, to consider both sides of issues, to figure out what makes us feel most satisfied. Reflection treats our critical thinking skills to a workout, refining them for easy transfer into other areas of our lives, including how we parent our children, situate ourselves for a promotion, or vote for the best candidate in an election. Becoming more contemplative through the process of journaling means living "for real," instead of just going through the motions. By exploring our thoughts through journaling, writers can stop detrimental habits and ritualize better practices for their health, their families, and their inner peace. Even the worst of times can be transformed into opportunities for personal growth by asking, "What was the lesson here?" If we don't think about something deeply, if we don't immerse ourselves in identifying and categorizing its layers, we won't understand it well. Living up to our true potential demands a high level of introspection, and journaling provides the framework necessary for reflection.

Chapter 6: Blessed You

*"When I started counting my blessings,
my whole life turned around."*

—Willie Nelson[57]

We humans are a superstitious lot. Some of us seem to believe that if we feel content with what we have and express appreciation, it somehow eradicates our desire for growth. In reality, gratitude doesn't dampen our ambition nor does it weaken our resolve to create the best life possible for ourselves and those we love. In fact, the mindset involved in recognizing your blessings can attract more of those good situations—more money, a beautiful home, satisfying relationships, and a circle of supportive friends.

Whatever you picture as an ideal life, one of the quickest and easiest ways to achieve it is making the shift to a mindset of abundance. As I grew up, good Texas mothers taught children not to say, "I'm full" at the table. It was considered impolite. In fact, my friend Judy Guerry told me about a southern aunt of hers who sidetracked this rule of etiquette by saying, "I've had a bountiful sufficiency." As an adult, I've come to relish the word *full*. My ideal life is full, full of family and friends, work I love, vacations that spark my imagination and renew my body and soul, and art that brings me joy. When I say *full*, these days I am speaking of the word in the same sense as my favorite Japanese word, *manzoku*, which means satisfaction or sufficiency—not just in terms of food but of being content with one's life, one's work, and one's progress.

At a particularly difficult and lonely time in my life, I girded myself by creating a mind map on which I brainstormed and categorized dozens of things I could use as a "happy fix" if I began feeling overwhelmed or depressed. I listed everything from listening to Cab Calloway's "Are You Hep to the Jive?"[58] to taking a hot bubble bath, from watching an old movie featuring Bette Davis or James Stewart to getting a "corny dog" at the local Dairy Queen. What I noticed was most of the things that I could honestly count on to pull me out of a bad mood in a flash were experiences I could easily create for myself. The knowledge that I could obtain bursts of happiness quickly and easily continues to buoy me in rough waters.

◆◆◆

My appreciation journals tend to be specific. I learned this from my grandbaby when she was two. When Isabella said grace before meals, her prayers were heartfelt. She was thankful for her "fishes," the Disney princess who caught her fancy, her mommy, and her new "bathing soup," a term which our family still calls our swimming costumes. She'd then end her prayers with "Happily ever after. Amen." I think she had the right idea.

My journal often takes my blessings as its topic. I try to avoid the broad and generic as I list the things I am grateful for. I'm not just grateful for my partner, for example, I appreciate that he has taught our grandchildren that they can be whatever they want and love whomever they want. I'm not just grateful for my father, but I'm thankful that he read "Snuffy Smith" and "Peanuts" comics to me every night, gifting me with a love of reading and humor.

What better could we wish for those we love than for them to be happy? I'm grateful that my father told me at 94 that he had enjoyed his life by saying, "It's been quite the ride!" I'm not just grateful for a good mother, I'm thankful for her ability to root for the underdog and to see the nobility in any human who crossed her path. I appreciate her making my favorite foods whenever I visit. No one makes beef stew or enchilada casserole like my mother.

I began experimenting with appreciation journals years ago, noting at least three things for which I was thankful each day. Sometimes I listed something as mundane as the way leaves had fallen on my car as I drove to work, a kind of red and gold rain. Other times I listed pieces of compliments I'd received or funny things I'd heard my students say during my workday. After appreciation became standard practice, I began feeling like the speaker in "Autobiographia" by G.E. Patterson who says, "I had everything and luck."[59]

Creating your ideal life isn't about hammering your desires to fit your reality, but it is about being on a frequency with abundance. It's about claiming the truth that you can "ask and ye shall receive."[60] It is about recognizing and verbalizing appreciation for things you want to be manifested more often in your life—moments of beauty, fabulous art, creative ideas, fine food, comfortable clothes, or encounters with kind people. When reading *Living by the Word: Essays by Alice Walker*, I tried to challenge her concept that what we pay attention to multiplies.[61] I started with lightning bugs, which I have loved since I was a child, playing in my grandparent's backyard in the Waco, Texas, twilight. I spotted one and then dozens and then enough that my husband and I stopped along a roadside to stand in the middle of a flock of fireflies where several got caught in my wild, curly hair. A couple of years later, I looked out at my new

Alabama backyard, where so many fireflies glittered in the sky that I wondered for a moment if some neighbor had strung twinkling lights in my trees. Yes, the things we pay attention to multiply.

Try this experiment in your journal. Ask for something in writing, believe that you'll receive it (a mustard-seed size belief will suffice), and watch it appear. I love the sound of church bells, so when I first did a manifestation experiment, I asked to hear more church bells the way I hear them when I'm in Europe. The next afternoon, my friend and I met for dinner in the local arts district, and bells sounded before I finished my first glass of wine. Yes, the bells rang the same time every day; I had just not previously been at that specific place to hear them. Skeptics will say these could be coincidences. Perhaps that's true, but establishing an intention to notice things made me more aware of the sights and sounds I longed to experience.

There are other instances when I can't explain my blessings, times when I am given something out of the blue that I'd been secretly wishing for. I loved and coveted a purple velvet fainting sofa I'd spotted in a Dublin apartment, and later at home my partner found its duplicate. "Somebody on our floor is getting rid of this," he said. "Do you want it?" Ummm, yes, yes I did. Sometimes, my blessings have arrived in the form of encouragement at just the right time or as a phone call from someone I knew in the distant past who I'd been missing. Sometimes blessings arrive as a chance to make some extra money right before I need to buy a birthday gift. Always, I am blessed with the knowledge that there will, for the foreseeable future, be enough food, books, and love. Once, during a particularly tight month as a young teacher, I had forgotten my lunch and knew my bank account would be barren and bleak until midnight when my monthly paycheck hit. I put a hand in my pocket and drew out a freshly washed twenty-dollar bill.

There will always be enough, and for that I am grateful. My assurance rests not on my point of privilege, although I certainly acknowledge that I have led a charmed and privileged life in every sense. My certainty comes from the truth recorded in my journals, the many accounts of events in which I received just the right thing at just the right time. It comes from the fresh perspectives derived by focusing on the positive and the good.

On a solo trip overseas when money was tight, I stayed in a hostel offering private rooms. I found myself thankful for a clean bed, for ornamental iron work on big windows overlooking a local park, for an ensuite bath with a tub in that land of tiny showers and shared facilities. Attitude made all the difference. I also think we usually get what we expect. Everywhere I ever visited, I have been met with kindness and courtesy, strangers willing to help with directions, and tolerant locals who aided me in navigating the post office lines and subway tunnels.

Feeling lucky and blessed is often just a matter of opening one's eyes. Are you under a roof tonight? Is there a musical instrument in your home? Can you hear your children snoring safely in their beds? If you felt hungry, could you make yourself something to eat right now? If you needed to walk up a flight of stairs or quickly run fifty feet, could you do so? If you are disabled or infirm, do you have the assistance you need? If you are confused, do you have helpers upon whom you could call? In your journal, list fifty of your blessings as quickly as you can and use this exercise as a jump start to developing the daily habit of gratitude.

♦ ♦ ♦

I don't want to give you the impression I have always had an appreciative attitude and waltzed through life. Like many people, I have been floored by heartache. I have experienced times I was dependent on others for rent money and knew the embarrassment of being fired from a job I loved. I have faced shocking betrayal by those I trusted most, and in such situations it is difficult to count one's blessings. Journaling became a lifeline to sanity during such harsh experiences.

Going through a time in my life I thought of as my darkest hours, I wrote almost constantly for nearly six months to make sense of strange events and plot twists I never expected and to keep my overwhelming sadness at bay. Little by little, the feelings abated, and blessings became more obvious. Even then, I had a family who supported me. Even then, I survived one day and another and then another. Even then, I was able to say, "Today, I am thankful for a body healthy enough to let me walk" or "Today, I am thankful for my sandwich at lunch and a clean, safe place to live."

In today's world, I wonder if a large percentage of our population believes there aren't enough blessings to go around as if by acknowledging someone else's expertise, we somehow diminish our own. As if by making sure everyone has enough to eat and enough money or resources to live in a safe home, we are somehow jeopardizing our own food security or ability to have a home suitable for our families. As if in providing healthcare to everyone in need, we'll somehow run the risk of not being able to visit our doctor when necessary. There is enough. A mindset of scarcity does not serve us well. It lowers our "money frequency," that attitude about money that allows it to flow to you and holding onto a fear of lack prevents you from wholeheartedly watering others from the deep well of your blessings. The pseudonymous author of 1 Peter 3:9 (NIV) teaches us that we were called to bless others so that we "may obtain a blessing."[62]

Seeded in childhood, attitudes of scarcity can be inherited. Parents' attitudes about money can be passed down. Did you or your parents grow up during the Great Depression when lack was the backdrop of many lives? Were anxieties about money discernable to you even as a child? Examining one's attitudes about money and shifting to a mindset of plenty can free you from unproductive stress and allow you not only to enjoy what you have but to increase your generosity to others. Once after making a big purchase, I worried that I had paid too much. My wise father shrugged and said, "If you can afford it, it's not too much."

Daddy also models an attitude of abundance. In his nineties, his body sometimes can't keep up with his spirit, but instead of complaining about being mostly housebound, he appreciates the fireplace in his cozy den filled with Western art, pictures of his family, and his new iPad, which he's on his way to fully mastering! Recently, hospitalized with pneumonia and sent to a rehabilitation center, he told me about a lunch he'd had—a cheeseburger. "They put bacon on it," he said, amused. "I'd never had a hamburger with bacon on it. It was *good*." He continues to recognize even small blessings. He continues to enjoy his life.

◆◆◆

Sometimes we sabotage our own blessings. We have a never-ending supply list that we must fill before we can allow ourselves to admit, "Right now, I have everything I need." Our motto has become: *More!* Our wellspring of want never seems to run dry despite our needs being met every day. The life of my wealthy relative was a lesson in recognizing blessings. She truly had all one could hope for, and yet, if she went to a nice restaurant she might complain that the silverware was too heavy or the perfectly cooked steak was too tough. If she was given two carat diamond earrings, she wanted three carats. If she had a nice car, she wanted a nicer and newer one. Consumerism attached itself to her sense of self somehow, letting her become a perpetually empty shopping bag that no amount of products, praise, or luxury could fill. Not being satisfied became her stock and trade as if it somehow made her classier or richer to be immune to the blessings around her. It didn't, of course. Her inability to enjoy her blessings simply made her dissatisfied during much of the long life with which she was blessed.

I loved her dearly and she was always kind to me, and I'm certainly not throwing stones as I have fought my own battles with being resistant to accepting and acknowledging blessings. I've labored under the misconception of "the starving artist," who suffers for their creative inspiration, believing for too long what the Irish poet Patrick Kavanagh said: "Luxury would ruin your sublime imagination in no time."[63] In reality, it's just as easy to pen a poem in a well-heated living room as it is to pen one in a cold-water flat. I can't stress enough how important it is to your success that you begin thinking of yourself as a lucky and blessed person. When you start tuning into that frequency, that godly channel that assures your needs will be met, you've taken a colossal leap toward preparing to build and receive your ideal life.

Life throws change at us again and again. Some change appears first as loss. Borrowed from a line of Naomi Shahib Nye poetry, a frequent writing exercise presented to my students is, "What have you lost that you still miss?"[64] Almost always, the people and items written about were blessings or symbols of blessings. Yes, you lost your knitted hat, but you still had your warm home, your coat, the grandma who had given that hat to you as a Christmas present. Fire consumed your home, but you still had a safe, clean place to stay that very night. You had friends who came to help you clear the debris or the means to help you rebuild. According to C.S. Lewis, "When we lose one blessing, another is often most unexpectedly given its place."[65] Loss sometimes appears to make room for new blessings in our lives. As the Persian poet Rumi wrote, "Perhaps God is clearing you out for some new delight."[66]

Embrace the truth that one of our greatest blessings is the ability to bless someone else. Living in abundance is a regenerating cycle you'll want to jump into as quickly and fully as possible. I heard a radio show about a woman who had lost her job. Her sense of worth went with the job. Looking for something that would pull her out of her self-defeating sadness, she recognized her talent for cooking and entertaining. She acknowledged the blessing that she had in food.

While searching for work, she began to invite others who were struggling for dinner one night a week. She credited this ability to care for others as having saved her from what would have been an emotionally exhausting period of her life. It made her feel better about herself to be doing something for others. No matter where you are in life, ask yourself, "What can I do for someone else? How can I be of service? Did every interaction I had with another person today make their life better or worse? Did I make those I encountered in my life feel seen and heard today?"

I am a firm believer that to be fully happy, we must live somewhere we love. I once heard a speaker talk about having moved away from the beautiful, clear blue skies of the Colorado mountains to the steamy, humid swamplands of Louisiana. Friends questioned his decision. Louisiana's muggy coastlands fed his soul, he explained. The Spanish moss hanging on trees made him feel happy. I questioned my parents' move from East Texas back to their home in Northwest Texas, a land my husband once described as "scrub and horizon," but the sense of space, the short mesquite trees, the big sunsets fed their souls and felt like home. They are happy there.

For me, as a lover of literature, having a view of a seven-story library that houses a copy of Shakespeare's 1623 *First Folio*, feeds my soul. It thrills me knowing I could walk across the street and check out a stack of books, just as walking into the small Red River County Library or the Bogata Junior High School Library of my childhood made me feel blessed. Overflowing bookshelves symbolize abundance to me. As a teenager, I felt blessed sitting on a swing on my parent's back porch, watching the sun go down. As an adult, I feel blessed sleeping under quilts made by women in my family, strong women who would have wished for nothing more than for me to be comfortable, warm, and loved.

Whether I have had sirens and other city noises or the howl of coyotes wafting through my windows, I have been lucky to live in places that sparked a sense of blessedness. I teach my literature students that in stories and books, authors often use houses as symbols for the people who live there. For example, Graham Green's Charlie from "I, Spy" whose father turns out to be a spy, lives in a house described as "irregular."[67] In your journal, explore what your home says about your life. Is it cluttered and chaotic or peaceful and well-ordered? Is it full of art you love or barren and minimalist? What styles make you feel best? Why? What objects give you comfort?

"God is in the details," Mies Van der Rhoe famously said, and your journal can capture the details that make your life pleasant or magical.[68] Look around the place you are sitting as you read this book. What details please you? What details annoy you but could easily be fixed? Could moving a piece of furniture, for example, clear up a cramped space that is a daily irritant? In your journal, start with the here and now. What do you notice and appreciate about the setting you have created for yourself? Continue embracing your power to determine, acknowledging freedom as you write about the setting in which you live, work, or write. Do you like the place you live and if not, what prevents you from packing up, selling out, and moving to an area that pleases you more?

We are a transient society. In fact, more and more of us have work-from-home jobs. There are fewer reasons for you to "bloom where you're planted" if you can't grow and flourish in that particular brand of soil. If a big move is off the table, what small things could you remove or add to make your environment comforting and stimulating, reflecting you and your personality?

I've learned a lot about living well from my friend Karla Schilling. On the outside, her home seems like any of the other suburban ranch houses on her street, but once inside I am transported into a world that is purely Karla—fashionable, comfortable, welcoming, surprising, and richly decorated! I am in awe of Karla's dramatic jewel-toned walls, her myriad antique crystal glasses, her abundance of candles, fresh flowers, and chandeliers—every detail reflecting a style I describe as "fancy gothic." Her home is a haven, not only for her but also for those of us lucky enough to make her guest list for the fabulous parties she hosts.

She has taught me that it is okay to make your home unique to your personality and style. In my old age, I've embraced my hand-me-downs: my paternal grandmother's buffet, my mother's 1940s dressing table with its round mirror, a flea market silver chest turned into a work of art with a new leather top hand tooled by my father, a hodgepodge of art I've collected, created, or been given by friends and family. I've developed my own style, a Bohemian, eclectic, cowgirl kind of style that rings true to me. I've never wanted a generic place, a place with no flaws or stories or surprises. Visiting Japan, I learned about the beauty of the Wabi Sabi aesthetic, an idea sprouting from the gold filling used to repair cracks in broken pottery, the notion that broken items can be transformed from a perfect state to something more appealing and beautiful not in spite of their flaws, but because of them.

Many of us have bought into the idea that our homes, like our lives, should be "normal." Why? We aren't all the same. Our uniqueness is a blessing. Our idiosyncrasies make us special. So, hang that inexpensive poster that sparks your imagination. Frame that strange picture that fascinates you. Pull out the photographs of people you love and who love you. Use the quilts your great grandmother sewed by hand from flour sack material and the afghan blankets knitted by your Aunt Nova. Break some rules to create an environment that pleases you; you are the one who lives there! In your journal, examine your place in the world, your community, your home. How does your home evidence your blessings?

A favorite pastor, my former student, Elder Roy Gaffney says, "Watch me turn up the blessing heat seven times!" In the world, there is enough! We simply need to share our blessings. America likes to call itself "the land of plenty," but it seems of late we have become stingy with our resources, our help, and even our compassion for others. In the pages of your journal, explore ways in which you could share the talents or blessings that you enjoy. As Edwin Markhem's poem "A Creed" reminds us, "All that we send into the lives of others comes back into our own."[69] What can you send out today?

♦ ♦ ♦

Journaling begets appreciation. It demands a call to attention. Keeping a journal can become a way of collecting good memories, generating awareness of the rightness of each moment in which you find yourself, and finding more peace of mind that will carry you to new levels of safety, security, and comfort. As a high school student, I was fortunate to read *Our Town* by Thornton Wilder. Its message resonated with me, awakening a more intense awareness of my blessings. As Emily Webb is struck by the memory of a book for postcards her mailman had brought her on her birthday, I realized how members of my own sweet hometown spoiled me in hundreds of ways.

I recognized early that the things we sometimes take for granted hold beauty and thoughtfulness we can't possibly deserve. Every single day holds something good, something amazing. Journals help us bask in the blessings that perpetually surround us. In your journal, start asking yourself, "What was my favorite part of today?" If you struggled today, start with: "I'm glad I was able to see. . . . I'm glad I was able to experience. . . . I'm glad I was able to have met . . . ." As Wilder put it, "We can only be said to be alive in those moments when our hearts are conscious of our treasures."[70] Use your sacred journal to acknowledge your treasures, your blessings, your full life, your "bountiful sufficiency."

Chapter 7: Spiritual You

"Re-examine all you have been told. . . .
Dismiss what insults your soul."

—Walt Whitman, *Leaves of Grass*[71]

There are as many paths to love, enlightenment, and understanding as there are human beings populating the earth. Some people consider themselves spiritual, but not religious. Others remain in one church, temple, or mosque most of their lives. Others have floated from one religious community to the next. The sublime and inspired books that pepper our spiritual journeys are plentiful, but engaging in journaling as a spiritual practice offers benefits to those seeking a way to be closer to their divine purpose as we study our own words, not the philosophies of others. Journaling opens writers up to the mystery of faith and the best parts of themselves as beings created in the image of God—whether one accepts that to mean an omnipresent entity or a metaphor for all that is good. Writing as a way to embrace our spirituality helps us examine our conscience, express gratitude, reflect upon divinely-influenced texts, engage in meditation, and—as Psalms 46:10 advises "be still and know . . . God."[72]

We can trace writing as a spiritual practice to ancient times. In the Middle Ages, for example, Saint Hildegard von Bingen used journaling, art, herb-based medical practices, and profuse letter writing to draw herself closer to the divine and to be of service to others. Modern journal-keepers can do the same, instilling in their journal, prayers, poems, and other methods of listening to a higher power, messages that often take the form of intuitive wisdom we carry within ourselves.

Moreover, John 1:1 begs exploration by any writer, any lover of language in all its forms. "In the beginning was the Word, and the Word was with God, and the Word was God," St. John, Christ's beloved disciple, scribed.[73] As a metaphor for Christ, the word *word* associates itself with power, truth, justice, and love. As a metaphor for the essence of a higher being, a creator of worlds, the word *word* defines writers when they are at their best, inventing characters, settings, and plots that carry our most heart-felt messages to the masses or simply to our own hearts. As we write a novel, a prayer, or a journal entry, we commune with that part of ourselves most akin to the great Creator. We touch and imitate the Word. We feel the power and miracle of language and expression, the sacrosanct nature inherent in the sheer act of storytelling. Through journaling, we can reflect upon, and rewrite our stories, recognizing as Brenda Ueland says, everybody "is talented, original and has something important to say," acknowledging our inherent worth as children of a higher power.[74]

Spiritually, there can be no better practice than to claim our sense of worth. Those who study great writers, artists, musicians, dancers, or engineers have often concluded that their subjects were no more or less talented than the regular hobbyist. The only difference was the experts believed their time spent studying and practicing in their fields was worth the effort to refine and perfect their work to the level at which geniuses toil. Journaling is worth the effort, and, equally important, you are worthy of journaling. Writing daily is not a time-sucking hobby, but rather one method to carve away that which harms us, distracts us, or repeats the messages that damage and defile us. We are the sculptors of our own souls.

◆◆◆

As we carve solid versions of ourselves, journaling allows us to encounter and converse with the most sacred elements around us. Our journals stand ready to nurse us to new levels of spiritual and emotional health. However, our progress towards such a goal can be hampered by negative messages about ourselves, messages we've soaked up from well-meaning families, thoughtless friends, conniving coworkers, or cheating spouses. In addition, we might be plagued by media images promoting unattainable levels of success or beauty. We might even entertain scars from religious organizations that don't honor our gender, our wisdom, our sexual orientation, or our talents. Journals invite deep digging. You can excavate the birthplaces of any self-deprecating messages on the pages of your notebook and leave behind hurtful or unhelpful teachings by trapping their source in the vault of your journal. While it's true journals often act as birthing centers for ideas and new goals, they can also serve as graveyards in which you identify and put to rest the beliefs about yourself that do not serve you.

Sometimes we lug about limiting thoughts about ourselves picked up from people who had their own issues—personal or professional jealousy, a weak self-esteem they hoped to inflate by deflating us, or a need to control us by diminishing the size of our dreams. They wrap these messages in statements such as, "Be practical!" and questions like, "Do you honestly think you can do that?" In your journal, acknowledge any negative beliefs you have about yourself and your abilities as they relate to your goals. Have you been told that "You're not the college type," that you "can't compete" with others (you don't have to), that you "can't do that at your age," that you should "just be lucky you have a job"? Sometimes these negative messages come tied with the pretty, but false, bow of "I only want the best for you, so I have to be honest."

Wanton criticism sometimes arrives disguised as care. Who needs that kind of so-called help? Of course, not all people who sparked the negativity we hold onto about ourselves meant us ill, but it does pay to think about the source of the information we allow to take root in our minds. Did that parent who didn't think you were "the college type" benefit from having you stay home to babysit your siblings or fear the destruction of his or her marriage once the last child left the nest? Did the co-workers who said you weren't qualified for the job really want those promotions for themselves? Did the teacher who disparaged your dreams and suggested you aim lower feel bad about her station in life? In your journal, analyze and put to rest messages about yourself that just might not be true!

Reprogram the tapes you have on replay in your head. If you always wanted to try something new, replace "I should have" with "I still can . . . ." Replace "If I were prettier or smarter or funnier . . ." with "Just as I am, I deserve . . . ." I believe in the power of affirmations. They are the psychological equivalent to "faking it until you make it." Hear something enough, tell yourself something enough, read something about yourself often enough, and you'll start to believe it. In this moment, only you can determine what you will or will not believe about yourself. Only you and God truly know you and that of which you are capable.

One message I often heard growing up was, "Don't crow about yourself." I was taught not to brag, not to get "too big for my britches," and never to think I was better than anyone else. Sometimes such messages teach us humbleness and give us a sense of equality and a heart for justice. Taken to the extreme, they can be twisted by our funny, little minds into "Don't acknowledge your gifts and talents," "Be afraid of appearing too successful or confident," and "Everyone else is better than you!" Today, in your journal, throw off some of these traps. Take hold of the tremendous life you were given.

Start your writing with a list of your greatest accomplishments. You don't think God would create someone without talents or beauty or abilities, do you? What do you do well? What are your greatest skills and strong points? Don't limit your answer to those someone told you that you should have. Start with the words, "I am smart enough to . . . ." Or, "I can still . . ." In your journal, brag about yourself! Go overboard congratulating yourself on everything you do well, on everything you have survived, on every achievement you have earned. Tell yourself, "I have the ability to . . ." Our journeys of accepting ourselves as spiritual beings made in the image of a loving creator often begin with realizing we are worthy of blessings. We deserve gifts. We merit self-acceptance and self-love.

We are God's highest form of creation. Shakespeare's dramatic hero Hamlet, even in the throes of his deep depression and disillusionment, exclaims, "What a piece of work is man!" He celebrates man's nobility in reason, infinite faculties, "express and admirable" form and movement.[75] Likewise, the psalmist writes, "I praise you because I am fearfully and wonderfully made; your works are wonderful, I know that full well."[76] What do you find wonderful about humans?

A healthy level of confidence is easier to reach once you come to terms with the reality that perfection is a facade. For years, I believed that I had to have all the answers, that I had to master every skill, that I needed to compete. Teaching reinforced this myth for me. I shut the classroom door, and—poof!—I expected myself to be a one-man band, capable of managing thirty-five students, individualizing instruction, healing the damaged, promoting literacy and a love of life-long learning, all while fixing broken copy machines. The reality is I was good at *some* of those things, but when I began accepting help from others, it became less important that I was perfect at any of my tasks! By their solitary nature or their competitive environments, other professions help engrain the same myth that to be successful in our fields we must master everything related to our job descriptions. Having opportunities to work with teams burst this myth for me.

For three years, I worked as a curriculum writer and trainer with Mina Davis, my good friend who could be considered my exact opposite in terms of temperament and personality. She is charismatic and detail-oriented whereas I am introspective and creative. She is extroverted and energized by crowds whereas I am an introvert who loves solitude as much as people. She is a "Do it now! Finish it early!" person whereas I can dawdle for a week toying with the initial brainstorming session for a project. Mina and I began to recognize, appreciate, and most importantly put to use each other's strengths.

Ultimately, our department went through a period of employment attrition that left us as a two-woman team. Working together, we performed small miracles, continuing to meet all our deadlines, churn out quality work, and assist and encourage the thousands of teachers in our district. I was free to create big ideas, to make curriculum theme associations and design engaging lessons while Mina easily managed to put the legs under my grandiose notions, share the product in brilliant trainings, fill the gaps left by my flighty nature, and make sure I met deadlines and got to meetings on time! It was one of the most productive periods of my work life, not because I was a perfect fit for the position, but because by recognizing my weaknesses as well as my strengths Mina allowed me to do more of the things at which I naturally excelled. Her personality and her gifts directly corresponded to the areas and skills in which I was shaky. We were better together.

Accept that you are only meant to be the perfect *you*, flaws and all. We sometimes labor under the delusion that we shouldn't admit to any weakness, to any lack of knowledge. A weight lifted when I began to study personality types. Valerie Sokolosky, author of *Monday Morning Leadership for Women*, taught me about the DiSC profile, the William Moulton Marston-inspired behavior assessment tool, centering around four personality traits—dominance, influence, steadiness, and conscientiousness.[77] I went on to study the previously mentioned Carol Tuttle's *Dressing Your Truth: Discover Your Type of Beauty*, which assigns a number to describe four energy types or ways of moving in the world, and Florence Littauer's *Personality Plus: How to Understand Others by Understanding Yourself*, which records her take on the ancient Greco-Roman medical theory of four humors presumed to correspond to four personality types—choleric, melancholic, phlegmatic, or sanguine.[78,79]

My journal record of these times overflows with the acceptances, acknowledgements, and admissions I made during each of those spurts of discovery. By accepting that I had one set of gifts and other people had another set of gifts, I reframed my weaknesses as ways in which the strengths of others could shine. I no longer feared not being the one who received the credit for everything, and I started finding myself saying more often, "I couldn't have done it without the help of . . . ." Friends, bosses, colleagues, and even strangers don't think less of you when you provide opportunities to let their talents be seen and their gifts unwrapped. Gaining the confidence not to be perfect can rocket us to new levels of spiritual growth, to lives in which we ignite the lights in others with a spark of our own vulnerability.

In your journal, keep an eye on situations in which you feel unable to ask for help and celebrate your willingness to let others have something you might have previously demanded for yourself—the spotlight in a meeting, the sole credit for a completed project, even a title at work. People who achieve don't do so by themselves. Who are people in your life whose ways of working or whose gifts are different from yours? How can you benefit from collaborating with those who outshine you in some areas? Who might need a thank you note for sharing their personality type and talents with you?

In your journal, consider any notions about independence that might have a stranglehold on your spiritual growth. What strengths and gifts do you use with ease? What weaknesses of yours could be the strengths of someone else in your life? How do you feel when you share credit for accomplishments? In what ways can you turn the spotlight over to another, blessing someone else by allowing them to use their gifts and talents? What would it mean if you recognized your short-comings and found ways to use your relationships with others to help you overcome the lack of those skills or personality traits?

◆◆◆

Our best spiritual selves shine through to others and come through for others. My colleague, Cyndi Dumas, explained her motivation for being disciplined in a daily yoga practice as knowing that if she took care of herself, reduced her stress levels, and was the best version of herself, then she could be of greater service to others. I believe our journaling practice can mold a better version of our spiritual selves. Journaling inherently makes us more aware, and that awareness can be used to notice, change, or celebrate some of the foods we eat, some of the exercises we engage in, or some of the relationships in which we participate. With the help of a journaling practice, we improve and heal ourselves so we may live our best lives—lives that allow us to serve others.

Likewise, a journal slows us down, allowing us time to think about all the ways in which we might make a moment or a lifetime better for another person. As we look inward, we simultaneously improve our outward vision, our understanding of where the call of service leads. In your journal, reflect upon how you can perform some act of service for someone else today. Service doesn't always take such forms as volunteering at a food pantry or homeless shelter. Sometimes we serve by saying to a quiet but thoughtful colleague, "What do you think of this idea?" or making sure you look lovingly into your children's eyes as you answer their questions, rather than keeping a constant eye on your cell phone or being distracted by work.

Sometimes, serving means listening. Sometimes, it is spending time with someone or listening to the same story for the fiftieth time and being just as interested as you were the first time. Sometimes, service means sending a card through the mail, leaving a batch of flowers on someone's porch, or sharing a meal with a lonely neighbor. Service can take the form of being a friend, offering a smile, giving a compliment, or asking a follow-up question. Saying, "You look so put together! Who taught you about fashion?" can start a lifelong friendship or make a stranger's day. Everyone loves a compliment, but a follow-up question can take a conversation to the next step, saying with interest, "I see you there!"

Living on the top floor of a high-rise apartment I got into the habit of instigating real conversations with random strangers and other residents while riding up and down the elevator. One time, I had to laugh at my own efforts. A young couple got on with two suitcases. They looked tired and a little angry at each other. "Did you go somewhere fun?" I ventured. "Kind of," the man said, offering no other details. "Here in the states or internationally?" I asked. "Chicago," the woman answered. They both continued looking forward, probably hoping the elevator doors would open soon and allow them to escape my questions. I waited a few seconds. "Business or pleasure?" I asked, grinning and laughing out loud at myself. Then, we all three broke into laughter. "I just had to ask one more question," I explained, and I told them about my habit of practicing deeper conversations. By the time they got to their floor, they were giggling and their anger at each other seemed to have given way to amusement at that crazy lady on the elevator. Even a quick conversation can sometimes be an act of service especially when we live in a world with technology that lets us communicate with each other more often but sometimes means we have less face-to-face interaction.

Spirit, Christ, the living light, the higher power, the unnamable, the Creator—whatever name you are comfortable calling God or the presence of goodness in the world—can speak through us to others by our willingness to *speak* to others! Never underestimate the positive power of simply making someone feel seen and heard. I shudder at the times when I diminished someone's day by being rude or impatient, and I repent the times I used harsh words or was enveloped by anger when kindness would have been so easy to offer. When we don't show empathy, our spiritual selves feel empty not to mention the potential negative effect our words and actions have on other people and those with whom they associate that day and for who knows how long thereafter. Journals provide a place to examine the ways in which we have interacted with the human beings who crossed our paths and to ask tough questions about what we contributed to their lives through our contact. Journaling also lets us celebrate the fleeting interactions we have with people, teaching us over and over that even these slight connections matter.

◆ ◆ ◆

Poet Paul Laurence Dunbar, the son of American slaves, explored the theme of suppressed pain and sorrow in his piece, "We Wear the Mask."[80] Ironically, the poem clearly displayed feelings that would have been too dangerous to present in other media. Without ever mentioning the words *Black, White*, or *oppression*, the speaker laid bare the emotions and situations that necessitated wearing a false face for the world. To use journaling as a spiritual tool, masks have to come off. We can and should dare to present our truest self to the pages, not the dressed-up version, exuding piety.

Unless we confront the rawest of our feelings, the most naked of our hearts, and the actions that haunt us most, journaling can remain an interesting past-time but never work its full magic on our lives. A lack of authenticity impedes our spiritual growth, confining our reflections to the superficial, and committing to our records the most surface of events without allowing us to delve into the significance of those experiences. Most importantly, it prevents us from changing our mindsets and habits, thus, preventing us from improving ourselves in any meaningful way.

In journals, we can ask ourselves how we can embrace truth even when it offers unflattering pictures of ourselves. We can take out our past and exercise or exorcise it on the pages. Learning, accepting, forgiving, and modifying our ways of being based on the realities and the lessons of the past becomes easier when we see our words, thoughts, and deeds transcribed in our notebooks. If reluctance raises its head, you might start an entry with the words, "I will never write about . . . ." The technique can provide a friendlier back door into the deepest recesses of your memories and knock the cloak of impossibility off your most far-reaching hopes.

I confess that one of the most difficult times to write is sometimes when I most need to be doing so. As one of my students recently admitted in her journal, "I didn't write for a while, but I was kind of not okay." Writing can help us sort through chaos, of course, but there seem to be times when we instinctively pull away from truth, fearing the full impact of facing whatever situation we find ourselves in. After such times pass, I always wish I had written more often, expressed more of my feelings, recorded more of the process of figuring out whatever puzzle life handed me. As Joseph Campbell stated, "The cave you fear to enter holds the treasure you seek."[81]

Finding myself reluctant to journal has become a red flag to me, warning me that I am, as my student wrote, "kind of not okay." If you, too, find yourself experiencing such a moment, you can try starting an entry with the words, "I don't want to write today, because I don't want to think about . . . ." Again, a backdoor works as easily as the front door for gaining admission into our journal. By making ourselves feel in control of what we are writing, by simply starting to list the things we don't want to say or admit, we are, in fact, facing our fears, and in light of spiritual growth, facing our fears is deemed a high priority.

Certainly, the Bible and other holy books teach us to "Fear not."[82] Jacob is told not to fear or to be dismayed and is assured that he will eventually have "quiet and ease, and none shall make him afraid."[83] In Matthew 10:31, we learn to "Fear not," because we "are of more value than many sparrows" upon whom God keeps watch.[84] And, most instructive is 2 Timothy 1:7, which reminds us that we have been given "a spirit not of fear but of power and love and self-control."[85] Likewise, Buddhist teachings hold that "The whole secret to existence is to have no fear," and Aristotle likened overcoming our fears with being truly free.[86]

Of course, fear is a natural human response, which can kindle our sense of alertness, keeping us safe. As we've previously acknowledged, sometimes there's a bit of the ancient in us that hearkens to the sound of a potential intruder or an unidentified shadow on the 'cave' wall. There's a difference between being safe because of readiness or vigilance and being immobilized by fear and, therefore, more vulnerable to the negative effects of *that* which we fear.

In your journal, list and explore your fears and their sources. Your list might start with spiders or snakes, but eventually get to criticism about your work. You might trace your fear of cats to secretly watching Jacques Tourneur's 1942 *Cat People* when you were a child.[87] You might also discover that your fear of water came from your grandmother's frequent telling stories about people who had died in a boating accident or drowned in a nearby pond.

Just recognizing our fears is the first step in confronting them, and being fearless is one of the qualities of a fulfilling spiritual life. Equally important is to examine how realistic our fears are in the context of our current lives. For example, how often do people fall from great heights unless they have dangerous construction jobs? What would be the worst thing that happened if you flubbed a big speech or took in a kitten? Sometimes our fears no longer fit us, especially those fears stemming from childhood experiences. If our fears are valid and would carry negative consequences, the journal can be the place to plan your escape routes, your solutions, your ideas for avoiding or overcoming the problem, situation, person, or things that kindle fear in you.

Journals can also be the place in which we exercise our abilities to assume positive intent and try giving people the benefit of the doubt. Are there situations that might change our reactions from negative to positive? By using our imaginations or by doing some casual research, might there be some room for a paradigm shift? A way to skew the way we interpret an event, a comment, or a reaction to allow for forgiveness? I realized I needed to engage in this broader way of analyzing and responding in my life when I met Katie, a senior high school student who arrived late to my 8 a.m. class. To make matters worse, she came in wafting a smoke smell behind her. "That Katie!" I said to myself. "How dare she show up late because she was enjoying a cigarette in her car!"

My attitude changed toward Katie after I read her first journal entry. She wrote, "I hate being late to class every day, but my shift at the Waffle House lasts from 5 a.m. to 8 a.m. I don't even have time to shower or change after I've cooked all morning, but I don't want to give up my job because I'm saving to take courses at the community college next year after graduation." I felt about an inch tall, thinking about how I had misjudged Katie and her situation along with her desire to do well and improve her life. Thereafter, I welcomed Katie warmly when she came into class as I should have done in the first place! I pre-set her desk with notes or instructions she might miss while she traveled from her job to our class. The new information changed my heart.

Perhaps, to move ourselves spiritually forward in order to be more loving people, we only need to assume reasons exist when we don't understand the behavior of others. Can I assume positive intent even without the benefit of a full story like the one I was fortunate to gain with Katie? In your journal, consider the ways you can offer grace to someone who appears at first glance not to deserve it, for as Hamlet points out to Polonius, if we were all treated as we deserve, "who should 'scape whipping?"[88] Instead of just complaining about someone else, whether that be their behavior or idiosyncrasies, journal about their possible reasons, guess the stories behind the person. What secret realities could spur the person's actions? How can you be the bigger person? As Buddha points out, "As the mother protects her only child even at the cost of her own life, in like manner is boundless, loving kindness to be cultivated towards all living beings."[89]

In your journal, locate those to whom you need to cultivate kindness, treating them as the spiritual and worthy beings they are even if part of you believes they "don't deserve it." Who can you protect in some way today? Whose dignity can you honor with your good treatment? When we hear the word *spiritual,* we might imagine a monk on a lonely hilltop communing with nature. In reality, our spiritual health demands human fellowship.

◆◆◆

Connecting with others presents us with the opportunity to serve, along with the equally important chance to be the recipient of service. John Steinbeck's *East of Eden* presents the healing of an almost lifelong strife between son and father when the dying old man humbles himself to ask for his son's help in taking care of him after a stroke.[90] Indeed, allowing others to help us can be a gift to them. Whose help do you need? In your journal, consider this and eventually consider all your important human connections. Who has given you unconditional love? What people energize you and make you feel good about yourself? How can you replicate what they do for you when you are with someone else?

Journaling can provide a place to keep and explore inspirational quotations, lines of poetry, and pieces of scripture. It is a place to collect and honor our own stories, to reveal the secrets holding us back from living our best lives, to interpret the experiences with which we have been gifted. Our truths, our lessons, our capacity to care, to understand, and to serve can all be enhanced with a focused journaling practice. Journaling allows us to make positive spiritual movements by paying attention. You obtained this book to become better, to have a better life, to achieve better outcomes for yourself and those you love. In the pages of your journal, identify the ways you fall short and rehash the scenes you've starred in today. How were you brave or heroic today? What was beautiful about you today? In what way have you experienced God's goodness today?

God shows up. I believe this in general, and I believe this is true when we journal with an eye toward creating a more spiritually satisfying life. Even the ill-fated character, Blanche DuBois asserts, "Sometimes—there's God— so quickly!"[91] When have you received messages, gifts, encouragement, or signs at crucial moments? When have your experiences extended beyond what conventional wisdom could explain? When have you realized, perhaps even years later, that you had made decisions that harmonized with a bigger plan for you in ways you could not have predicted then? In your journal, consider how your talents and passions have been used for service, how they can be further used, and how you can become someone E. L. Konigsberg refers to as "vessels for the divine"?[92]

Your life's journey takes a route no one else has mapped out. So, too, will it be with your ability to engage in sacred journaling. So, too, will it be for your spiritual path. No one's course is straight. No one's way is entirely smooth. Commit to remain in the process. Nourish your soul with the words you write and with the wisdom that comes through as ink on your pages.

Chapter 8: Visionary You

"I went to the woods because I wished to live deliberately,
to front only the essential facts of life,
and see if I could not learn what it had to teach, and not,
when I came to die, discover that I had not lived."

—Henry David Thoreau, *Walden*[93]

Living deliberately super charges your life. Too many people seem to settle for "just the way things turn out," rather than to make the daring and purposeful choices that bring them closer to happiness and fulfillment. In his book, *The Power of Now: A Guide to Spiritual Enlightenment,* the modern philosopher Eckhart Tolle writes, "It is not uncommon for people to spend their whole life waiting to start living."[94] Repeat after me a mantra I use: this now is it. This moment is all we have!

A number of years ago I went to a party and met some old friends. We laughed, drank, danced, and reminisced. Then, I ran into a friend I'll call Amy. She leapt into a diatribe about how she was going to be relieved when the remodel on her house was finished. Construction took longer than expected, but when she had her new kitchen, she'd be able to relax and be happy, she said. Others passed off her comments as being her way of sharing her pride of ownership or the financial success she had achieved or just being her way of catching us up with what was going on in her life. I flashed back to other things I'd overheard her say in the past. "I'm going to be happy when it's summer!" "I'm going to be happy when I finally graduate college!" "I'm going to be happy when I get a second degree, when I get married, when I have a baby, when I get a promotion." There was always some finish line, standing between my friend and happiness. I wish I could have shared with her what I want to emphasize to you: *this* time is all we have.

Amy had been waiting to be happy all her life, and I suspect when we are both in our dotage she'll be rocking in a chair in the corner of her perfect kitchen saying, "When I'm in heaven, I'll be happy." Well, I'd rather not wait! I'm more of a "rage against the light" person, as Dylan Thomas would say, and I suspect you are too, or you wouldn't have picked up this book. We've talked about recognizing your blessings as a way of being happy in the present moment, but now let's devote some time to upgrading your life even more!

♦ ♦ ♦

Oprah Winfrey once advised people to "Create the highest, grandest vision possible for your life, because you become what you believe."[95] What grand visions for yourself did you have as a child? Did any come true? Are you still hanging on by a thread to some of those lofty plans? What would your life look like if your dreams came true? Take those questions to your journal, and in it begin to sculpt a clear vision of your best life. I urge you to let nothing prevent you from drafting this vision in your journal today—not naysayers, not the critic in your head, not the bad advice from a high school counselor, not the mother-in-law who wants you to spend more time with the children, not the pile of work waiting for you at the office, nothing!

In books such as Napoleon Hill's classic, *Think and Grow Rich* and Rhonda Byrne's more recent *The Secret*, we read about putting into practice the concept of manifestation.[96,97] Many people of faith dismissed such notions as New Age hocus pocus, but in John 16:23 Christ assures us that if we "ask of the Father in [Christ's] name, he will give it to you."[98] For me, the practice of manifestation is a Biblical truth. Mark 11:24 says that when we ask for something in prayer and believe we have received it, it will be ours.[99] Luke 11:9 and Matthew 7:7 echo each other saying, "Ask, and it will be given to you; seek, and you will find; knock, and it will be opened to you."[100]

Why then do we fail to ask, or why do our wishes and desires fail to manifest? Christ explained this as a lack of faith. Philosophers explain that you must believe in the reality that the Universe will provide. It's human to doubt, but doubt lies to us about our capacities and lives within us to deter our dreams. Believe in your dreams, form that mustard-seed size faith, and make it snowball until you are able to say, "'Move from here to there,' and it will move, and nothing will be impossible for you."[101] Nothing will be impossible for you! Savor those words. Bask in that affirmation. Write it in your journal. We censor our dreams with inklings of uncertainty.

In your journal, let go of some of the ways you have put limits on your life and on yourself. You might begin with the words, "I came to believe it was impossible for me to . . . " or "I came to understand it wasn't realistic or practical for . . . ." When you complete this writing, you might find that many items in the journal assignment need to be realigned to the vision you have for yourself. Dream big! If you are a person of faith, ask yourself, "What is impossible for God?" If you are a skeptic, research others who have achieved a dream similar to yours. Are they really that different from you?

As you begin the journey of creating, recreating, or refining your vision for your life, consider those around you. Do they encourage or try to suppress you when you speak aloud parts of your vision? Why? Does it serve them if you remain where you are, living a "less than" life—less than that of which you are capable, less than equal to what you want, less than your divine purpose?

During the process of establishing your vision, begin surrounding yourself with people who believe in you and who *won't* consider your best possible life out of reach. Make a list of people who will support you on your journey—those from whom you can learn, those who love you, and those who you could better serve. Be prepared, though, to make changes to this list with time.

Having started a pop-up art-themed dinner business, I was surprised when one of my dearest friends, a person who supported similar events and art organizations throughout our city, failed to purchase tickets to any of the events I planned. I was flabbergasted and a little hurt, so I called my mom. In a second career, my mother put together a formidable sales team, and when a new member of her organization was struggling to persuade her family members to try her products, my mother explained to them as she also explained to me, "Yesterday, you weren't, and today you are." As Jesus explained, "A prophet is not without honour, but in his own country, and among his own kin, and in his own house."[102] Beware those who aren't willing to adjust their small vision of you when your grand vision takes hold! You don't have to give up their friendship but realize that some folks will be unable to update their perception of who you are and where you are heading! Sometimes, those who do not have preconceived notions of us are more willing to support our efforts or put their faith in our proposed expertise. People who have always known us in one role might think of us as an amateur when we begin a new venture.

When I teach community college students, especially students from urban neighborhoods in which going to college is not the norm or when I have older students who are returning to school after having made their living in a different way, I always remind them of the phenomenon of "crabs in a bucket." There's no need to put a lid on a bucket of crabs, because when one crab begins to climb out, which is a relatively easy task for a crab, the other crabs begin to pull the climber back down. As you start to envision better for yourself, crabs in your life might say, "Is that investment smart at your age? Aren't you afraid of flying overseas by yourself? Don't most people usually make it in that field when they are older . . . or younger? Aren't you scared about losing your steady income?"

My favorite red flag, alerting me to a potential crab who might try to pull me down is, "What does your husband think about that?" It's a comment that tries to suggest that you will lose your marriage if you make it big or spoil yourself with a splashy purchase or participate in a meaningful trip or an expensive training. It's a comment that tries to say, "You have this, so you shouldn't want that" as if your success or happiness were in jeopardy or as if there are only so many blessings allowed in our lives. We don't have to give something up to get our prayers answered. God isn't sitting around like a gameshow host saying, "What will it be? Will you give up the trip to Tahiti to receive the surprise under box number two?" We don't have to forgo our dreams to keep all that we love about our current lives.

In your journal, if you are toying with an idea or an element of a vision you've held in the back of your mind and are wondering, "Why haven't I already achieved the big goal?" then you might need to recognize the other "crabs in your bucket." Are there people whose opinions and comments are holding you down? They only have the power of the crab if you agree to give it to them. You're not a crab. You are a human being, the creator's masterpiece. Others can't pull you down if you choose not to stay in the same old bucket.

◆ ◆ ◆

When we have a precise vision, we know where to focus our energy. There's an old joke about the God-fearing man who prayed for rescue from a flood. He listened to the broadcast warning to evacuate his area, but he said, "God will save me." His friend came by with a car and begged him to leave, but the man said, "God will save me." Waters continued to rise around and inside his house until a rescue boat was sent to his door, but he refused to leave saying, "God will save me." He sat on the roof of his house, the only place waters had not yet reached, and a helicopter came by. Again, he turned them away saying, "God will save me." Ultimately, the waters rose too high, and he drowned. In Heaven, he said to God, "I had faith! Why didn't you save me?" God says, "Man, I sent you a warning, a car, a boat, and a helicopter! What did you want?" I believe our prayers are answered in many ways, but when it comes to making a vision a reality, we must accept the help or act on the inspired idea.

To move closer to my vision, I've begun to carve out my life in five-year segments. Ten years would be too long for this exercise. When I think in terms of ten years, it gives me the false sense that I have lots of time to finish a project or achieve a goal. Five seems to season my plans with just the right amount of urgency. Anyone on a job interview has probably been asked, "Where do you see yourself in five years?" In such situations, we wonder what the interviewer wants us to say and try to hammer our answers to fit. But in a journal, no one is judging you based on your answers. Where do you want to be in five years? What experiences do you want to have? What characteristics or skills do you want to have developed? What job do you want to hold? Where do you want to be living? How do you spend your weekends and free time? Who is around you? Use these questions in your journal to continue honing your vision. Then ask, "What can I do today to take one step toward that vision?" What can you do with the next five years? How will you have served others? How will you nurture yourself?

You may wish to spark your vision, using a backwards design process. A home-ec teacher gave me a slightly morbid assignment—to write my own obituary. At first, I was turned off by thinking of my impending death, but I quickly realized the value of the work. In your journal, write the article that might be printed in a newspaper upon your death. At the end of your life, what do you want to be said about you? Who will mourn your death? What will you have accomplished? What will your major contributions have been? What education will you have earned? Writing from this point of view helps you get your priorities straight, celebrate what you already accomplished, and make plans for reaching your remaining goals with the time you have! You *are* the author of your own story, and no matter what stage of life you currently find yourself enjoying, now is the time to write the best chapter.

In my journal, after many pages of exploring my vision and exploring my reasons for wanting certain things, highlights of my five-year goals include: publishing two books and visiting two of the big locations on my travel list—the Taj Mahal in India and the temple ruins near Angkor Wat, Cambodia. I also listed a vision of what I want to do for my partner, his grandchildren, and my parents. I have a vision of what I want my volunteer work to look like and who I want to help with my work.

I also have a broad chart with the next thirty years mapped out roughly in five-year boxes. That, too, fills me with motivation to enjoy and accomplish what I want to while I can; time is short! Now, my grandmothers and some of my aunts have lived well into their nineties, so I hope to have much more time. For now, I'm focusing on the next three decades. Make your list with the decades you hope to be your most productive, healthiest, and most able-bodied. You might be writing about your 20s through your 40s or your 70s through your 90s. In this thirty year chart, I list the places I want to go, projects I hope to accomplish, and blessings I want to bestow on others.

The items on such charts do more than provide a list of tasks to tick off during a certain period. Together, they help me form the overall vision of the person I am. I am a world traveler, a loving person, a writer. Who are you?

♦ ♦ ♦

When we compare great leaders with those who have failed, often the secret to success began with a clear vision. What does your ideal life look like? What do you want? What do you love about your current situation that you would prefer to retain over time? What gives you pleasure? What benchmarks have you established for yourself that will let you know you are on track for making the most of your time on earth? Explore these questions in your journal as you begin to visualize on paper the way you want to be. A vision doesn't *just* contain interim deadlines or endpoints, although your plans for manifesting your vision can contain checkpoints and can even start with the end in mind. A vision is not just a magical gift registry or a bulleted list of accomplishments. It, too, is about lifestyle.

A month from becoming a young wife in Northeast Texas, I wrote about what I wanted in my first grownup house—green plants, throw pillows, candles, books, and fluffy rugs. Since that time, I've re-envisioned my home many times. As an adult, I've lived in eleven cities and home has meant everything from a revamped old one-room schoolhouse to a new suburban construction below a beautiful, protected mountain to an artsy somewhat-dilapidated apartment in a two-story pre-Civil War house to an apartment in a downtown skyscraper. In each place, I've reiterated and expanded upon that first journal description of what I wanted for my home. Writing about how I wanted to create my personal environment has helped me produce the home I desire.

Journaling helped me define what I needed, what was beautiful and inspiring in my home, and what I wanted guests to feel as they entered it. As I came home from work evening after evening, home became my sanctuary, but without the clarity of journaling I might have fallen prey to the expectations of others—my friends with suburban mini-mansions where extra rooms and garages reign or city friends with decorator-planned rooms. Instead, for me, home has meant an eccentric collection of old family pieces and hand-me-downs and art I've made myself or purchased from local galleries. Journaling about how I wanted to live, about what was important to me, or about how I felt about particular pieces and items has helped me cull useless or painful possessions and collect more of the things that give me pleasure and spark inspiration.

Writing about what we want provides clarity. It signals to us and the universe that we value certain things. It helps us create our grocery list for happiness—not just in terms of material accumulation or domestic surroundings, but in terms of our purpose, our habits, our relationships, and our careers. Writing down what we want in our lives helps us start working toward those goals. As Rhonda Byrne says in *The Secret*, "What you think about you bring about."[103] Journaling your thoughts is one way of acknowledging, ordering, and when necessary, changing your thoughts. The way to kickstart your ideal life is to visualize it!

I still ask myself, "What do I want?" My answers have changed over the years, and because of the writing I've done I've been able to create the kind of life I want for myself and my family. "What's next?" I ask myself. "Where do I need to put my energy?" I'm not sure that I agree that an unexamined life is not worth living, but I do believe examining one's life and where one wants to be— what one wants to achieve and experience—can direct new energy toward the ideal life one wants to craft.

◆ ◆ ◆

Writing what you want has more to do with getting it than simply clarifying your goal and helping you reduce the clutter that would keep you from focusing on that goal. Some believe that the words on the page themselves send a message to the universe that help you begin to attract or manifest what you want. And, indeed, like art, handwriting on a page is an expression of ourselves and our humanity. Our written expressions, our words on a page, often contain information that comes straight from our most inspired voices, which is not to say I also don't write a lot of less than good things. My journal is full of less-than-meaningful bits of drivel, but occasionally in my journal, I find something wise and true that I otherwise would not have articulated, a message that I would not have listened to had I not written it down.

Having grown up hearing verses such as, "Ask and ye shall receive,"[104] I believe in requesting what you want and expecting to get it. Whether you believe it in terms of prayer or the iteration of asking the universe and manifesting it, writing down what you want is a technique that works. In your journal, write often, starting with the prompt, "What I really want now is . . . ." Create the shopping list you want presented to you by the universe or Spirit or God or whatever you choose to call the positive energy that infuses our lives. Be specific. Ask for what you want. Ask for it on paper. What are twenty-five things, trips, items, or experiences you want? Don't overthink it. Just let your thoughts fly.

Words on pages are valuable and magical. We no longer have to keep our books chained because they are priceless works of art, because the printing press has made literature, history, and philosophy something all of us can access. Handwritten words on paper are an extension of our personalities, proof of our existence like the red painted hand of a caveman on a dark wall. It is a bit of everyday magic that sends the message to ourselves and to those who come after us that in this moment, I am. I think of the scene in the movie version of *The Color Purple* in which Celie is sweeping her kitchen and finds the word *sky* on a piece of wax paper and the power of finding her sister's letters to her stowed away by a selfish husband.[105] I think of Muslim cultures who prevent the recycling, shredding, or pulping of worn copies of the Quran, but rather bury or burn the text in a respectful fashion. Words are everything. With words, with the precision of language, there is little we can't create, do, or express.

This, I believe, so I sit down and write, "I am this. . . . I will have this. . . . I will create this. . . . My life will include this . . . ." And, more often than not, what I write about eventually turns up in my life, in my circle of friends, or in gift-wrapping. So, pick up that magic pen (It's the one nearest you!) and write your list as if you were a child writing to Santa at the height of your Christmas belief. Write your wishes as if you had discovered a magic lamp. Today, in your journal, stop dividing things into *wants* versus *needs,* stop thinking about what you can or can't afford, stop censoring your desires because what you really want to be or do or see doesn't seem reasonable. You deserve an abundant life.

♦ ♦ ♦

When we envision our lives, we must imagine more than those things we desire to own, the possessions that would make our lives easier or more luxurious or more beautiful or comfortable. We must talk "lifestyle" in our journals. My favorite actress Myrna Loy once said, "They say the movies should be more like life; I think life should be more like the movies."[106] I thought of this on my most recent trip to Paris as I sat in the front of the Palais Garnier where I made chit chat with a lovely French stranger seated next to me on the maroon velvet chairs as we awaited a ballet to commence. I think of that moment as the most far away I have ever been from my parents' comfortable Rosalie home just outside the city limits of Bogata, Texas, where I sat on a wooden swing watching sunsets. The extremes of my life have been blessings. What extremes have you experienced? Celebrate those movie-worthy moments in your journal or describe the elements of life you want for yourself, that you might think of as befitting only a movie star. What scenes do you want to participate in? Begin creating your life story, scene by scene.

In your journal, recall the movies that have inspired or thrilled you. I did so want to be Myrna Loy, drinking champagne on New Year's Eve with tablemates ranging from monied socialites to those just returned from a stint in jail for petty theft. I wanted to be a writer, working on a story that would save a man's life, edited by a charming Cary Grant. I wanted to be Doris Day, wearing sunny yellow sweaters or sleek white evening gowns, trying on fur coats with linings that matched my dresses, hats, and gloves. Most of all, I wanted to host dinner parties, rounding up a group of fascinating people to talk and laugh with while candles flickered on the table.

Those fantasies shaped my vision, so that today, I'm just as likely to know the name of my homeless friend at the corner as I am my state representative. Just as my movie idols did on the screen, I gather my friends around my table and laugh and talk about the most interesting subjects. I wear whatever makes me feel wonderful, and I write to help my fellow humans create their visions and live their dream lives. Proverbs 20:5 says, "The purpose in a man's heart is like deep water, but a man of understanding will draw it out."[107] Allow your journal to become one of the tools that draws out the purpose already planted deeply in your heart.

◆◆◆

In your journal, you can sculpt a broad vision and you can also fill in the details. Drafting a life list, a catalog of your "must-dos," can help you flesh out your vision, putting some sturdy legs under your wild dreams. What are the top hundred things you want to do, see, or experience during your lifetime? I have found this brainstorming exercise to be incredibly helpful. As I go back to a list I made more than eight years ago, I see that many of the objectives I listed have been met! You can think of it as a bucket list of a hundred things you want to accomplish before you kick the bucket. But, I like the term *Life List* better. How are you going to live your life? What special events, memories, or achievements will be the hallmarks of your life? What daily comforts will you gift yourself?

John Lennon is attributed with saying, "Life is what happens to you while you're busy making other plans."[108] Action is important. With my high school students I try to explain how quickly time passes, how I was thirty and the next day forty and the next day fifty. As I look back, I see some decades and some years were more productive than others, more joyful or disappointing. One thing is certain: when I am clear on what I want, I get more of what I want! I make more progress in the direction of the things I've set for myself as desires, dreams, and objectives.

With my students, I provide a structure, asking questions to help create a well-rounded list that will encourage them to sample some of the entertainment, travel, literature, and art that life offers. You are welcome to answer the questions in your journal! Focus on what you want to do with the time you have left on this earth, if the questions don't spark a hunger in you. I ask what sporting event students want to attend, what foreign cities and domestic locales they want to visit, what opera or ballet they want to see, and what other things they want to experience or learn. I always include wildcards: a secret dream they had that didn't fit into other categories I'd given them. I invite you to make such a list.

First, I start with literature. Mrs. Barbara Russell, my high school teacher and Dr. Gretchen Mieszkoski, my graduate professor, both assigned memorizing the first lines of the Prologue to Chaucer's *The Canterbury Tales* in Middle English. I butchered the recitation both times, but the words were in my head when I finally made a pilgrimage to Canterbury Cathedral and paid homage to "hem hath holpen, whan that they were seeke."[109] They were also in my head in an urban middle school setting when I experienced a strong case of spring fever and simply wanted to wander away from that place and that year of such utter disappointment. The lines reminded me that what I was feeling was nothing I wouldn't live through. They reminded me that there were still many beautiful things and people among the sacred and the profane, all interesting and worth noticing. Poetry can help see us through rough times. I was grateful for those teachers who made me memorize poetry.

On my first trips to Ireland, I was amazed by the conversations in which an Irishman would insert a recitation of a few lines of poetry that were perfect for the moment and made a point in his argument! I vowed to learn more poetry, to memorize lines I wanted to keep. I remember the late Senator McCain, with whom I disagreed on much but for whom I held tremendous respect, talking about staying sane during his days as one of several American Prisoners of War. He and his fellow captives shared and taught each other everything they had ever learned by memory. What "good stuff" do you want in your head? Write it in your journal on one side of the page, and explain what it means and why it is important to you to learn it on the other.

My friend, David Stoops, shared with me a system for filing poems by month. Every year, he adds new poems and reflects upon old poems that fit the season, the mood, or the challenges of each particular month. Often, the poems that make it into my files begin as cut outs or printouts from magazines or other sources, little items that I have pasted into my journal. Others I remember from school or find in books of poetry I leaf through in bookstores or at home. The poem "Invictus" contains two of my favorite lines, "I am the master of my fate, / I am the captain of my soul."[110] As you craft, revise, or upgrade your vision, remember like a child taken to the candy aisle with a lenient grandparent, you can have anything you want. Don't let life pass you by! Don't wake up with another decade having passed and nothing new checked off your "someday" list. Make your time count! As the poet Mary Oliver asks, "What is it you plan to do with your one wild and precious life?"[111]

Chapter 9: Flexible You

"Change is the law of life."

—John F. Kennedy[112]

Ａll change—even positive change—produces stress, but journaling can help alleviate the stress of change. By reviewing my journals and my life over several decades, I've come to believe that my fears about most changes thrown my way were unfounded. The changes I didn't want, the changes I would never have chosen for myself, turned out to be openings for greater joy, faster advancement, and more happiness. Many people simply hate change, but as every fan of *Star Wars* learned from Shmi Skywalker, "You can't stop the change any more than you can stop the sun from setting."[113] Change affects us from the moment we take our first breaths until the moment we "shuffle off this mortal coil."[114]

Dealing with change, then, becomes the essential element for being happy for even in a life we create with intention, even in a life most would consider ideal, changes arise. Our mobility and strength deteriorate with time, we lose loved ones, friends move away, the economy ebbs and flows and with such shifts our financial success can suffer or benefit.

Many years ago, when a series of major changes were slapped upon me against my will, I learned that no matter what, I would be okay. Bad things happen to us. You can experience illness, grief, unemployment, betrayal, or sudden loss, but you *will* be okay. That doesn't mean life will ever be the same, but at this moment, you are okay, are you not? You are breathing. You are safe. You have the time and ability to purchase and read a book, to write a page, the time to consider what you want out of this life.

No matter how badly a moment affects us, we can persevere. We can sustain and sooth ourselves in the worst of times by going back to being present in the moment, acknowledging our blessings, and clarifying what we really want as we go forward. Again, this attitude of mine comes not from a point of privilege, although I fully admit that I am privileged in every sense of that term. However, I honestly believe that nothing could steal my overall happiness again. I have bad days and challenging encounters, and I face the same trials as everyone else, but I have learned as Maya Angelou said that while "Stepping onto a brand-new path is difficult," nothing is "more difficult than remaining in a situation, which is not nurturing to the whole woman."[115]

As you journal, you become aware that you have ultimately always been okay. You have survived crises, pulled yourself up, and switched directions many times. Journaling, then, reinforces your understanding that even if the present is blissful, change is inevitable and it's our ability to cope with change that determines whether we can be happy. Flexibility remains the best shock absorber when dealing with obstacles in our paths.

◆ ◆ ◆

I have lived a charmed life. The only child of parents who deeply loved each other and me, I spent my youth in one small community, an area in which friends became extended family. My upbringing provided many advantages from which I continue to benefit to this day, but it did not prepare me to be flexible in my approach to life. Many times, I have felt that Mary Shelley was correct when she said, "Nothing is so painful to the human mind as a great and sudden change."[116] Like you, I have been thrown unexpected curve balls, and my own ability to switch on a flexible nature hasn't been an instantaneous process. With the assistance of journaling, flexibility has eventually kicked in, called me to action, and kept me going, not always along the same route as before but always moving forward.

Journals can record events, feelings, and your analysis of a situation, but in order to employ the writing process as a therapeutic tool, users have to focus on the present and the future more than the past when facing change. Writing again and again with nostalgia for a situation that has passed does not allow you to move toward a more satisfying life in spite of a challenge or loss. Memories should give us support, teach us lessons, or provide understanding, but they should not be filtered through rose-colored glasses that help us remain stuck in an emotionally negative place. In the Jewish tradition as an allusion to Proverbs 10:7, those who have lost loved ones are sometimes told, "May their memory be a blessing." I believe this statement should be a guiding force in your journaling practice. If reliving a memory does not bring clarity or comfort, move away from that memory, and write about the present or the future.

This advice does not negate the usefulness of the journal as a therapeutic or psychiatric tool. There certainly will be times when a journal helps you get bad feelings or experiences out of your head and onto paper, giving you a vantage point from which you can view them more objectively. But, please, understand that you don't always figure out the reason behind every change immediately, and sometimes there simply isn't an answer. Even when there is a purpose or a lesson, it can be years before the answer shows itself to us. Being flexible is simply another way of saying you have developed resilience and emotional strength, which is not to say you should not feel every emotion associated with, for example, the grieving process.

However, it does mean, you ultimately hang on to the knowledge that if you have lost a person who loved you, that person wants you to go on living and being as happy as possible. Poet Pablo Neruda wrote to his potential widow the instructions to "survive [him] with such sheer force / [she] wakens the furies of the pallid and the cold."[117] In continuing as best as we are able at each stage of the grieving process, we honor the souls of those who have passed on. Being able to handle ambiguity might be the key to coping with a life full of "slings and arrows" and a "sea of troubles" as Hamlet would say.[118]

◆ ◆ ◆

Certainly, we experience a stream of negative and positive events during our lifetimes. Such is life! While there is much within our control, we must also look down the barrel of situations in which the only thing we can control is our response. It sometimes helps to clearly identify each loss for what it is—change.

Years ago, I experienced an unexpected breakup that suddenly changed my expectations for my life, my work, my living situation, and my family. I felt devastated, demeaned, and a little depressed. As I got myself together and worked out what life was going to look like, I stayed with my aunt and uncle. For a few days, my goal was simply to get through the day and crawl back into bed. In an effort to cheer me up, my uncle called some younger friends of his to take me out when I heard him say, "She's broken up with her boyfriend and is feeling sad." Hearing those words put my experience into perspective and became a turning point for me.

What had happened to me except a change? The breakup felt life-shattering at the time, but ultimately, it was a necessary step in finding the life I was meant to live, one with a partner who supported my writing efforts and invited me completely into his family. Sometimes, we bask in a sense of "specialness" when we are victims. We think, "No one else has experienced this level of betrayal or unhappiness." I remind you again that almost everyone has experienced something we might not be able to bear. Other women and men have lost spouses and jobs, faced transfers when they didn't want to move, been the victim of unspeakable crimes, faced the loss of a child, struggled with money, survived abuse, dealt with health problems, and experienced legions of other hardships.

It is not my intention to suggest that you dismiss depression or other mental health issues, and I do not mean to suggest that one can hop through the natural stages of grief at warp speed. But, it is always worthwhile to remember, others have experienced whatever you are experiencing and survived. You will, too. At the end of your page in which you cry out in pain, you may wish to write these words: "Others have survived this experience. I will, too." In this way, if you are writing about loss in your journal, you simultaneously begin training yourself to focus on your resilience, not the trauma. You are not what happened to you.

When trying to live your ideal life, flexibility can make all the difference. Flexibility's value can be seen when the other car cuts you off, when the grocery store is out of the one ingredient you need, when you don't get the promotion you wanted, or when life seems to have pulled the rug from under you. Part of living well means having the emotional resources to adapt to disappointment and to make a Plan B. Flexibility doesn't mean changing your goal, necessarily, but it might mean varying the route you planned to take to reach that goal. As a writer, I'm reminded of J.K. Rowling's having said that "rock bottom became a solid foundation on which [she] rebuilt [her] life."[119] Living in poverty, she finished the first of her *Harry Potter* books only to have it rejected by twelve publishers. When Bloomsbury finally said yes to the book, Rowling was given only an advance of £1,500. Obviously, that was just the start of her literary and financial success as *Harry Potter* went on to make Rowling the richest author in the world, according to *MoneyInc.com*, which reported her net worth to be over a billion dollars.[120]

To succeed, we need the flexibility to deal with our failures as obstacles, not stopping points. If we can't get to where we want to go one way, we need to reroute ourselves. While bedridden for months and no longer able to stand and create his vivid paintings or fabulous sculptures, Henri Matisse began experimenting with painted paper and scissors. Thus, began one of his most productive periods as an artist, during which he produced *Icarus*, possibly his most famous and recognizable work.[121] A black image of the boy plunges from the cobalt sky, and we see his wing-shaped arms flying as if he were dancing, not drowning. Although Icarus' dream of flying to freedom failed as he splashed into the sea, the Matisse interpretation of the character shows us the marked beauty of our own hopefully slower-paced journeys toward death. He urges us to recognize, record, and dance among the starlit moments of our lives, no matter how temporarily we are allowed to participate in this process of flying. Blocked in the production of his art in one way, Matisse found another avenue to expression.

What failures have you endured that eventually led to new discoveries about yourself and your capabilities? What parts of your past do you tend to romanticize? Is this harmless and pleasant, or do such memories keep you from fully enjoying the current moment? In what ways have you been blocked from the route to success and happiness you have mapped out for yourself? Are there other ways to get where you want to go? Who has achieved what you want to achieve? What was the process for that person? In your journal, interact with your past to uncover times when you stopped a trip rather than found another route. Reflect on your emotional and intellectual responses to change. What might you do differently next time when faced with a distraction or a disappointment that threatens to leave you despondent?

Each time I travel, I experience a reminder that rigid thinking only produces regrets, sorrows, and unnecessary stress. Planning a vacation is part of the fun and establishing a loose agenda can save time on the ground, maximizing the time you have at your destination. However, I traveled once with a consummate planner who was an inexperienced traveler. Inevitably, wait times were longer than she predicted, trains were slower, and items on her agenda had to be marked off. Experienced travelers know this is just part of the process, but for my detail-oriented friend, the trip was a failure. Each day, she called her family to report what she *hadn't* gotten to see or do, sometimes spending more time on that description than on all the wonderful experiences she had been able to fit into her day.

Part of travel and part of life that makes it satisfying is the surprise, the gift or interaction we didn't expect, the opportunity to try something new. Americans in Europe frequently misinterpret slow service at local cafés. If one is handed their check too soon, you might be getting the bum's rush, not quick attention from a competent waiter. Instead, if you are well liked at a restaurant, you are allowed to linger, to enjoy the view, to write in your journal, to chat with your tablemate for as long as you wish. When you are ready for the second glass of wine or a check, eye-contact is the only alert your waiter will need. In these languid moments over a coffee or a meal, it is the surprise that is satisfying, not the view of the landmark close by, but the visiting choir that breaks out in song, the snippets of conversation, the light touching of another's wrist in candlelight. Flexibility leaves room for such sights. Don't misjudge your reality as a mistake without taking a moment to look for the silver linings. What have you overlooked? What do you see and hear at this moment?

♦ ♦ ♦

Too often, we settle for situations that are comfortable, but not happy. This is because our thinking and behaviors have become immutable. In settling, we prevent change from leading us to a better place. Fear holds us back, and we ask ourselves, "What if the next thing is not better?" The truth is the very next thing might not feel better immediately, but if you have left an environment that hinders you or if you desire more than your current situation offers you intellectually, emotionally, or spiritually, you are on your way to a more enriching life. In your journal ask yourself what changes you need to initiate to improve your life.

Even those who have crafted their ideal lives don't live in some beatific Neverland. New challenges arise daily, but journaling can prepare you to face them with a sense of optimism and confidence rather than dread and stress. When my granddaughter was two, she found my worry dolls, small fabric dolls in a wooden box, the idea being that one whispers worries inside the box, and the dolls absorb our worries for us. It's a nice idea, and I admit that my superstitious nature kicked in when I saw Isabella playing with the little dolls outside their container. "Isabella, that's not how these dolls work," I explained. "You have to keep them in the box so you can tell them your worries. Otherwise, they let your worries out." She kept playing and said reassuringly, "It's okay. I'm not going to *do* worry." I thought that was a fine philosophy to live by, and I decided not to "do worry" either!

Whenever we must plow through a change or challenge, worrying about what is to come is not productive. Instead, you can write in your journal, "I know

I can handle this change, because I have already . . . ." We too often keep our failures close to our heart or at the forefront of our consciousness, but we are less comfortable discussing and owning our successes. Make a list of things you have achieved. They needn't all be grandiose accomplishments like hanging by your fingertips on a Rwandan mountaintop during a gorilla tracking expedition or making a speech to a stadium full of people.

Perhaps, you started a new exercise program or piano lessons? Have you diffused a conflict that could have ruined a friendship or made someone laugh? Keep thinking of small and large accomplishments. Think of this page as a kind of grown-up permanent record and read and add to the list often. This is no time to be modest. Remembering your past successes helps you address new challenges with more certainty in yourself and your ability to adapt and thrive.

Success is not always ascending. The never-ending path toward one's idea of perfection often feels like we're taking two steps forward and one step back, and it doesn't always run in a straight line on flat ground. Journal entries remind us that we have been successful in the past, and we will again. Likewise, journals provide a place for us to prepare to breathe before acting when faced with difficulties.

♦♦♦

It's equally important to learn to be flexible in your expectations of yourself. Perfectionism can rob us of our joy and stop us in our tracks before we've truly given ourselves a chance to fly. The art of creating a more flexible you lies in becoming more comfortable with being less than perfect. Journaling reminds us that we are human.

With each new decade added to my age, I've become more comfortable with not being perfect. In fact, I've often been fairly comfortable with sometimes making ridiculous mistakes. At a crowded conference once I had slept late and dressed quickly. I had sat through the first session and then walked through the conference hotel when I heard a panicked woman saying, "Ma'am! Ma'am! Stop!" Then she whispered to me in a serious and urgent voice, "I believe your shirt is inside out!" I was amused at her level of concern. "Thanks for telling me," I said. "Oh," she whispered in an even-more serious tone, "I would want someone to tell me." I had to laugh. She was much more embarrassed for me than I was for myself. In fact, wearing my shirt inside out might not even have been the biggest mistake I'd already made that day! I went upstairs and made the shirt right-side-out, but what pleased me about the encounter was my confidence, the fact that I needn't be horrified by a mistake.

Don't let your fear of being wrong or making an error, keep you from living your dream life. A mistake might, in fact, be a necessary first step! Similarly, don't let not being perfect keep you from the work you are passionate about. The Scottish researcher, Sir Alexander Fleming was notably careless in his lab habits, but instead of holding him back his haphazard cleaning routines led to the discovery of penicillin. Tradition holds that Fleming failed to throw away a culture plate and returned from a two-week vacation to discover that it had been contaminated by a mold which was, in fact, dissolving the bacteria around it.

The juice secreted by the mold was later found to be effective against all gram-positive pathogens, including those that cause meningitis, scarlet fever, gonorrhea, diphtheria, and pneumonia. Aiming for perfection in ourselves is a grand idea, but sometimes it's our flaws and imperfections that lead to our greatest contributions. Be flexible with yourself. Give yourself grace and grant yourself full permission to be imperfect. Have your flaws ever contributed to something positive for yourself or for others? In your journal, explore your imperfections in a new light.

When I was ten, my sweet grandmother, Veda Mayo Black, bought me a book used in the charm schools of the old Montgomery Ward department stores. The gift taught me to put all my skirts together, all my pants together, all my blouses together, separating each category with a long ribbon tied with a bow to the rod on which the clothes were hung. Later, as an adult, another book taught me to organize my clothes from the darkest color to the lightest with all my browns, pinks, reds, yellows, purples, and pinks together. I'm good at neither of those systems! Instead, I hurriedly clump all my laundry in the closet, skirts mixing recklessly with pants, forest and rose and taupe and azures mingling unabashedly!

No doubt, the charm-school teachers and contemporary closet organizers would be aghast, but I've discovered amazing outfits by having a less-than-picture-perfect closet. My hot pink and bright orange combos were striking long before Taylor Swift brought them to the red carpet. My jeans paired with the frilly, feminine white blouses I always associate with poets were textbook texture mixing. Allow yourself to recognize that you might be subconsciously choosing to be less than perfect for a reason. How does your imperfection serve you?

◆ ◆ ◆

Inflexibility finds its origins in fear as do so many other negative traits, but being fearful is not the same as being careful. For example, responding sensibly to physical dangers or contagious illnesses is not the same as being afraid. Fear suffocates and stops us, whereas wisdom extends our lives and ultimately expands our joy and satisfaction. In 365 different verses, the Bible counsels us to "fear not."[122]

Creating and living our best lives requires making changes, leaping into the new without a net or a bridge back to the old. Forming a more flexible relationship with our current lives means not just tiptoeing out of our comfort zones, but running full speed while realizing we might first hit a brick wall that sends us reeling! However, when we have identified our purpose, our passions, our vision for ourselves, and the way we want to live, even such shocks can lead us to the next step, the better way, the more perfect approach that lets us soar to the heights for which we were created. Fear not.

How often have you stayed stuck because changing was too great a challenge, too uncomfortable, too problematic? Have you remained in an environment that didn't serve you or in which you couldn't serve others because moving on felt too cumbersome or financially or emotionally dangerous? We have to face hard decisions with an unfaltering belief that we will always be okay. If we change our lives once, we can do so again and again until we have what we want. You don't have to be unsettled if traveling from town to town or country to country is not your thing. Just change yourself, and your circumstances automatically change.

Many of my best adult friends have chosen to remain in the same communities or neighborhoods in which they grew up. You don't have to move to a new house or instigate a divorce from a less-than-perfect-for-you partner unless you want to do so. You can be flexible within any framework you choose. It is perfectly fine to stay put in a job you like, in a relationship you want to keep, in a home you find comfortable, or in a town that offers you every opportunity to help others using your skills and abilities. Change is no more valuable an end goal than maintaining the status quo.

At the heart of journaling is the practice of telling yourself the truth with abandon. Veracity and honesty must be constants in the writing we do for ourselves. Otherwise, we are working in fiction; we are spinning tales that attempt to hammer our deepest desires to fit our current realities rather than to challenge ourselves to change the course of our lives so we can meet our best selves. With a commitment to absolute truth, use your journal to ask what big changes you need and want to make? What small ones . . . ? How can you alter your current situations to look more like the ideal life you crave? Clutch that life that you might have held as a secret, a life that might have been stifled by people or—more often than not—by our inability to truly believe we deserved such a life and could make it so!

I remember reading a short story in high school and fearing that I could already relate too much to its main character, Louisa. In Mary Eleanor Wilkins Freeman's "The New England Nun," Louisa has been long engaged to a man who left the area fourteen years ago to make his fortune. When he returns, she views him as a disturbing presence in the meticulous house she keeps and a disruption to her rigid routines. She gladly forgoes the marriage to maintain her current way of life.[123] As a youth, I read the story as a sad tale about a woman who lacked the flexibility to allow another person into her world.

As an adult, I read the story as being about a woman who had carved out her version of an ideal life and had the wherewithal to scoop up an opportunity to retain it. Unless what you choose is harmful to yourself or others, your vision does not have to match what society decides is the norm. Release yourself from time frames that someone else dictated. I never read the articles, for example, that tell me what I should have gotten rid of or purchased by a certain age. When I told my mother I'd be in my fifties by the time I finished my last degree, she just looked up and said, "What age will you be if you don't finish your degree?" A wise woman!

In your journal, ask yourself if there are areas in your life in which flexibility is needed? It's true that without a flexible nature, we might never experience the moments that bring us the greatest joy. We must also be willing to put in the energy to retain the people, places, and situations that do allow us to feed our souls and grow. In your journal, explain how you will tap into the discernment to know what should stay or go as you make your next move on your spiritual, emotional, social, and intellectual journey. If you had wandered only the first road you planned for yourself, what sights and scenes would you have missed? How has flexibility served you?

Charles Darwin reminded us that "It is not the strongest of the species that survives, nor the most intelligent. It is the one that is the most adaptable to change."[124] Too many people, when faced with a rejection or obstacles, change their goals, reduce their expectations, or worse, give up. Journaling can keep us focused on our passions and our end goals, and it can help us create new plans to achieve those goals as often as necessary. When you face a barrier, change your route or adapt your plan, but do not change your vision. Be clear about what you want, but be flexible about how you will obtain the life you desire.

Chapter 10: Focused You

*"Your destiny is to fulfill those things upon which you focus
most intently. So choose to keep your focus
on that which is truly magnificent, beautiful, uplifting, and joyful.
Your life is always moving toward something."*

—Ralph Marston[125]

As we continue to absorb and apply the Buddha's statements that "We are shaped by our thoughts; we become what we think,"[126] and Proverbs 23:7, which similarly teaches us that, "As one thinketh in her heart, so is she," our journal helps us gain control of our thoughts and, therefore, our behavior and outcomes.[127] Journaling produces greater focus. Focus produces greater results.

Intellectually, we know these truths, but distractions are bountiful in our modern world. E-mail, texts, a twenty-four hour news cycle, children who need chauffeuring, and work days that no longer begin at 9 a.m. and end at 5 p.m –so much vies for our attention in today's typical week that the best of intentions don't stand a chance!

If we are to have an ideal life, we must develop the ability to say, "I won't be able to do that" whenever we face activities that would be less than constructive, productive, or enjoyable for us. What are your distractions? What habits fill your days that don't move you to the next level in your journey to your ideal life? In your journal, spend a page recognizing those tasks that plague you, the things you do that don't necessarily contribute to your ideal life. What events or activities suck your time without providing an equal financial, emotional, spiritual, or intellectual reward? To what have you said yes when you should have said no?

Someone else *will* plan the gala if you don't. Someone else *will* organize the car pool, host the annual luncheon, or read your friend's latest fanfiction piece for typos. Juggling a thousand things doesn't make you a better person than anyone else! In fact, it probably means some vital things aren't getting the full attention they deserve, or you aren't getting the time to focus on the activities and people you value most and the tasks that will move you closer to your dreams and your most fulfilling life. Don't sabotage your future by refusing to say no to things that don't align with your vision!

"If you're not financially independent," advises author Gerry Roberts, "you shouldn't even own a television!"[128] We might all be shocked if we kept an account of the hours we spend watching editorialized news programs or inane comedies, feeding ourselves material that doesn't challenge, teach, surprise, or truly amuse us. If we spend those hours working toward a goal, being fully present for our children or our partners or parents, or using our natural talents, imagine what we could accomplish? I'm not against television, but I feel that it's our civic duty to pay attention to global, national, and local events as reported by an unbiased news source. How many of our evenings are spent in front of the television, instead of reading a book, reaching out to our friends and family, or taking the next step to building our successful careers, a comfortable home, or a better world? Beware the screen that steals an intentionally lived life. Journaling demands that you take a good look at how you are spending your time. What habits are defining your life? How close is the way you currently live to your dream life?

♦♦♦

Sometimes, we fall into the trap of believing that being busy is being productive. If your ideal life revolves around staying occupied or running lots of errands, then checking off boxes might be just the thing. But, for most of us, our ideal lives center around a goal associated with using our talents and experiencing more of what we consider our grand purpose. Those goals are rarely accomplished in our spare time unless we make them our area of focus. Zig Ziglar once said, "I don't care how much power, brilliance, or energy you have. If you don't harness it and focus it on a specific target and hold it there, you're never going to accomplish as much as your ability warrants."[129]

My partner, Gary, splurges each year to enjoy one of his passions; he holds season tickets to the Dallas Mavericks' games. When we began dating, I often found myself taking the train to the stadium with him and watching a basketball game. Now, I love an occasional game, but most of these dates were preceded by a full day of work, a quick change of clothes, a hurried dinner, and a tremendously stressful effort to beat the clock in order to make it to our seats by tip off. Inevitably, by the time I climbed the stairs and sat down, I was exhausted. When I discovered Martha Beck's article, "Twenty Questions that Could Change Your Life," I found myself sitting in the stands mumbling, "Is this really what I want to be doing?"[130]

I love the Mavericks, and their current owner, Mark Cuban continues to amaze me with his acts of charity for the city of Dallas. However, being at a game was rarely what I wanted to be doing. I'd have much preferred having the game on television as I sat in my recliner, enjoying my downtown view, writing in my journal, and drinking a glass of wine while lounging in my pajamas. When I finally started suggesting that Gary invite another friend, my quality of life improved. I think his experience improved, too, as those he invited were always delighted to get to see a live game and could talk to him about the intricacies of the sport or the wisdom of player trades in far more depth and with much more genuine enthusiasm than I could muster.

In what ways can you carve out more time to do what you need or want to do just by saying no to the things you don't enjoy? What do you do frequently that you don't have to do and don't want to do? Think about how you spend your days hour by hour, and in your journal take a deep dive into answering Beck's question, "Is this what I want to be doing?"

Recently, Maxine Waters, a US Representative from California, made famous the expression, "reclaiming my time," when she interrupted Treasury Secretary Steven Mnuchin's long-winded answers designed to limit her questions during an exasperating hearing process. I'd buy the t-shirt with that slogan! We all need to be able to use that philosophy if not the actual phrase in our daily lives. In what ways can you "reclaim" your time? Are there activities that can simply be marked off your calendar? Are there easier ways to accomplish some of the things you feel you must do. Could you save time by buying a robot vacuum, hiring a cleaning service, using laundry services that offer delivery, ordering gifts and groceries online?

I know that some people find household chores soothing, so understand that I suggest these particular steps as someone who has never answered "yes" to the "Is this what I want to be doing?" question with a broom or dust rag in my hand. You might be thinking such luxuries are too expensive, but is the investment in accomplishing a bigger dream worth it? How many hours would delegating these responsibilities or outsourcing your household maintenance gain you? What are the steps you need to take if you are to marshal the mindset, possessions, and relationships needed to become your most genuine self? Most highly successful people habitually take risks, listen to their hearts and intuition, and tune out the naysayers and defeatists. Is your big goal pushed to the side or squeezed into the tiny cracks among everything else you do? How much of an investment are you willing to make for your dream life?

Avoiding mental clutter and filling my life only with items that are beautiful or useful to me help maintain focus. In your journal, consider a time period or a work project during which you felt extremely focused. What circumstances made this level of laser-sharp attention possible? What took a back seat during this time in order for you to work at your best? Start a page with the words, "My productivity toward my ideal life or major goal would skyrocket if . . . ."

Not everything that takes time is useless. While I currently enjoy the benefit of an easy ten-minute commute, I once worked in an Alabama city forty-seven miles away from my house. I happily stayed in this position for ten years, but the hours I spent on the road were pleasant. Traffic was light, and the foothills of the Appalachians provided daily delights as the seasons changed—bunches of golden rod in the fall, an owl perched on an oak fence post as my car passed, the kudzu-covered remnants of an old barn, steam rising from the land like ghosts in the winter, and in the spring? Colors to rival those of the Easter Bunny's best basket.

My imagination was constantly stimulated by these natural sights. Moreover, the ride before work gave me time to plan my day, listen to language tapes to prepare for my next trip, predict and prepare for challenges, and rehearse my presentations. The drive home after work let me reflect on what I had accomplished and what I could have done better. It also let me catch my breath before coming home and hurling every mundane detail at my husband, who'd had his own full day at the office. In other words, rather than needlessly consuming my time, the commute helped me accomplish my goals in several areas of my life. My drive helped me whittle down my focus to the things truly necessary in each area of my life.

To live our best lives, we must have time to "sit under a tree and think" as I once heard E.L. Konigsburg say. When designing your life and determining how you want to continue moving towards the targets your journal helps you shed light on, remember to insert into your schedule, time to wander your favorite trails or to daydream. In your journal, address how you will renew and relax. What habits do you need to form around sleep, exercise, and medical care? Being healthy and well-rested helps you focus, allowing you to be at your best intellectually and emotionally as well as physically.

Certainly, writing in our journals helps us sharpen our focus. Like many creative types, I'm a bit of an old crow. I'm easily excited by any bright and shiny idea or commitment. I want to do everything that sounds fun! If time allowed, I would learn a dozen new languages, volunteer at every organization in town, join a new club, view every new exhibit in the local museums, and attend every gallery opening. If time allowed, I would continue my piano lessons and start three new businesses at once! Time, though is short. In studying those who achieve major success, I've found that they have one thing in common: they place their energy on one thing. In today's parlance, they consider it their brand. For me, whether I'm teaching or writing my next book or traveling, my focus is on journaling and helping others use journaling to improve their lives.

A few years ago, I experienced a particularly creative period in my life. Ideas bombarded me! Before I could start one project, another intruded. Before I could finish writing one story, the plot of another began knocking on the door. I tried to do everything! I wanted to write this, paint that, travel there, host this. Ultimately, I made a list of all the projects and pursuits flying around my brain. Astonishingly, there were more than forty on my list—many more than I could think about in a given day, much less complete! No wonder I had begun to feel a bit overwhelmed! Are you also juggling too much?

Making the list of ideas worth pursuing helped me honor my innovative brain and shelve, without guilt, the projects not aligned to my true passions. Instead, I moved to the forefront those ideas that supported my vision of myself and my finest life. While I value the ability to have an influx of creative thoughts and to make connections between ideas, ultimate success comes from completing projects and seeing our ideas through to completion.

I've benefited from focusing on only one big goal in each area of my life. For me, these categories include family, spiritual growth, friends, writing, and health. What are the major areas of your life? Journaling—that process of dreaming, planning, rehearsing, reflecting, and evaluating—provides an anchor, keeping us attached to our largest dreams and our ideal lives despite other distractions.

I pull out my journal at many different times of the day, but others value a more structured discipline. My friend, author and professor, Kate Mele, journals in the morning with coffee brewing and a candle burning. Others write before going to bed, laying down the events of the day and previewing what the next day will bring. If your day is filled with putting out fires, responding to the whims and needs of children, and juggling a variety of other responsibilities, blocking out journal time in your calendar will be vital to doing the word work that leads to your most satisfying life. As Colet Williams often reminds me, "It's time to make the thing the thing!" Writing is my thing, but no matter what your passion or purpose is, writing in your journal can help you carve away at the superfluous duties we've needlessly assigned ourselves. Journaling will establish your priorities and help you select the one goal you want to accomplish first!

◆◆◆

While journaling can and should be used to write our way into clarity, it should not be used as a medium for wallowing in our stresses whether they be people, situations, or events that make us too busy, worried, or anxious. When we ruminate over our stress, we don't reduce what ails us. It is fine to acknowledge how you are feeling in your journal, and you should do so. However, when your practice becomes only describing the amount of stress you're currently under, you aren't using your journal for its true purpose, which is to say, you aren't diminishing the power of your stress but rather reinforcing it! If I ever said I work better under stress, I lied.

What I probably meant was that having put off a task until the last minute, I had no choice but to finish quickly, releasing myself from crippling perfectionism. The reality is that chronic stress kills brain cells and shrinks the prefrontal cortex, the part of the brain most associated with our memory and our ability to learn. In your journal, ask yourself, "How do I want to improve myself today?" Use your pages to create and recreate life goals and to-do lists for those events and projects that would otherwise feel like too much. Journaling can convert our jumbled thoughts into clear strategies that make greatness manageable, moving us out of the mediocre and mundane one doable step at a time!

In your journal, meditate upon your first turning point goal, the key word in your personal mission statement, the significant contribution or accomplishment at the forefront of your vision. Write that word, decorate it, doodle, or illustrate around the word. Allow yourself to savor thoughts related to your success. Focus. Pray. Visualize. Then, journal again! Refine and expand your vision, remembering to focus on life as you want it to be.

♦ ♦ ♦

As we go forward, we can ask ourselves, "What do we wish we could tell our younger selves?" Sometimes, that is the advice we still need to hear. For me, the answer has become more and more clear. I'd make sure the younger me understood the importance of never letting anyone else establish my goals for me. I still struggle with letting others influence me by listening when they say, "You should . . ." or "You'd be good at . . . ." A journal perpetually allows me to return to my vision and goals, my secrets and dreams. A journal allows you to take control over your life in ways you might never have experienced. Journaling reminds you that even when you have no control over a particular situation, you can always control your response. Are there systems or people in your life trying to tell you a story about yourself that doesn't feel right? In your journal, you can rewrite such tales. Recommit to the self-selected good life you have written for yourself.

Journaling helps us control the voices telling us we can't, we shouldn't, or we won't. The words on paper that describe our ideal lives keep our internal censors at bay. In your journal, as you write, you protect yourself from settling for less than you deserve, and because journaling helps you get to know yourself and crystallize what you really want, it helps shape your future. You silence negative opinions whether they come from others or from some place within yourself. You acknowledge the blessings you enjoy and the positive ways in which you can excel each day. You list your achievements as a constant reminder that you are, indeed, making progress. Focus improves as I declutter my schedule and reclaim valuable hours in which I can focus on the next priority, the one that steers me to the next level in a life about which I once only dreamed.

Facing my journal, I feel the presence of a built-in accountability partner, reminding me not to postpone my "real" life but helping me maintain focus and release those elements transform my vision into my reality. Alone with my journal, I solidify a connection with the divine and view myself as a created being born with passion, talent, and a purpose in this world. In the pages of my journal, I have met myself and experienced what Aristotle called "the beginning of all wisdom."[133] I wish you the same gift as you continue your voyage towards the life you have always wanted. I wish you the power of words.

Acknowledgements

I wish to thank my parents (I sure got lucky in that department!); Judy King, my aunt and an extraordinary reading teacher; and Brady and Shirley Black, who let me hang out and journal myself to a good place one hot summer in Waco, Texas.

I am thankful, as well, for the blessing of amazing teachers from first grade through graduate school, along with my many current and former teaching colleagues and friends. One great teacher can change a life but having the benefit of a long series of fabulous educators in your life can help you move mountains!

For their support of my writing and living my best life, I thank Patricia Tennison and my Paris Café Writing tribe.

This book was truly a team effort! For creating and sharing the beautiful piece of her Hippie Cubism art for use on the cover of *Sacred Journaling*, I am grateful to Ramani Urbiztondo. Likewise, I am thankful to my El Centro student-turned-friend Ray Davidson who gifted me with a photo session by the talented Chantz Hough.

And, for their tolerance with me whenever I said, "Let me just finish this paragraph first," I thank Isabella Marie and Kennedy Medina and their grandfather, Gary Bates, who shared them with me.

About the Author

Leilani Barnett is an author, educator, world traveler, and social activist who has used journaling successfully in classrooms and workshops for more than 25 years. She holds a Bachelor's degree with a double major in English and journalism and Master's degrees in literature and educational leadership. Currently, Leilani is completing a Ph.D. and expanding her international writing workshop tours through WritingAdventures.com.

Leilani lives in Dallas, Texas, with her family and her beloved chihuahua dog. She teaches American literature at a private Catholic school and leads a meetup group for authors called Write Now.

Her work has appeared in *English Journal, Wanderlust: A Travel Journal, Perceptions, The Westchester Review, "Alabama English, She Speaks: An Anthology of Women's Voices,"* and other publications.

Leilani is also a frequent speaker on the topics of writing, traveling, and journaling. She has been a workshop leader or speaker for the Institute of International Education, the National Council of Teachers of English, the International Reading Association, The Alabama A&M National Writing Project, the Toyota International Teacher Program, the Texas Writers Guild, and other organizations.

A journal-keeper since she began forming words on paper, Leilani has experienced first-hand the benefits of journaling her way to a life full of service, deeper spiritual practices, satisfying work, and enriching relationships.

Leilani invites you to subscribe to her website at WritingAdventures.com and follow her on Twitter, Instagram, and Facebook @WriterLeilani.

Notes

One: Writing You

1. L'Amour, Louis, *Education of a Wandering Man: A Memoir* (New York: Bantom Books, 1989), 126.
2. Julia Cameron, *The Artist's Way: A Spiritual Path to Higher Creativity* (Los Angeles: Jeremy P. Torcher/Perigee, 2016), 9-16.
3. Anaïs Nin, "The New Woman," *Ramparts Magazine*, June 1974, 42, https:// www.unz.com/print/Ramparts-1974jun-00037/
4. Luke 4:24 (American Standard Version)

Two: Mistake-Proof You

5. Simone St. James, *The Broken Girls* (New York: Berkley, 2018), 331.
6. Michael J. Gelb, *How to Think Like Leonardo da Vinci: Seven Steps to Genius Every Day* (New York:
7. Delecorte Press, 1998), 76.
8. Natalie Goldberg, *Writing Down the Bones: Freeing the Writer Within* (Boston: Shambhala, 2005), 6.
9. James Joyce, "Eveline," *Dubliners* (New York: Penguin, 1956), 37-43.

Three: Free You

10. Albert Camus, *Conférences et Discours 1936-1958* (Paris: Gallimard, 2017).

11. Geoffrey Chaucer, "The Wife of Bath's Tale," *Canterbury Tales* (Fort Worth: Holt, Rinehart, and Winston, 1989), 121, line 905.

12. Frances Scott Key, "The Star-Spangled Banner," *American and Commercial Daily Advertiser* (Boston), approximately 17 September, 1812, line 8.

13. Latrobe Carroll, "Willa Sibert Cather," *Bookman*, May 3, 1921, https://cather.unl.edu/writings/ bohlke/interviews/bohlke.i.15

14. Shelley, Mary Wollstonecraft, *Frankenstein*. (Penguin Classics, 2012)

15. Millard Kaufman, Bowl of Cherries (London: Atlantic, 2009).

16. Harriet Doerr, Stones of Ibarra (Kbh.: Gyldendal, 1985).

17. Wallace Stevens, "Thirteen Ways of Looking at a Blackbird," poets.org, 1954, https://poets.org/poem/thirteen-ways-looking-blackbird

18. Jack Canfield and Janet Switzer, How to Get from Where You Are to Where You Want to Be: The 25 Principles of Success. (HarperCollins Publishers, 2007).

19. Janis Joplin, "Me and Bobby McGee," www.youtube.com, accessed January 15, 2022, https://www.youtube.com/watch?v=sfjon-ZTqzU.

20. Kaylin Haught, "God Says Yes to Me," Library of Congress, Washington, D.C. 20540 USA, n.d., https://www.loc.gov/programs/poetry-and-literature/poet-laureate/poet-laureate-projects/poetry-180/all-poems/item/poetry-180-126/god-says-yes-to-me/.

21. Sandra Cisneros, "Born Bad," *The House on Mango Street* (London: Bloomsbury, 2004), p. 61.

Four: Secret You

22. Jean Racine, *Britannicus* (1669), IV, 4.

23. Graham Wallas, *The Art of Thought* (London: Jonathan Cape, 1926), p. 102.

24. Flannery O'Connor, "Quotation," www.goodreads.com, n.d., https://www.goodreads.com/quotes/315733-i-write-because-i-don-t-know-what-i-think-until.

25. Bessel van der Kolk, The Body Keeps the Score: Brain, Mind and Body in the Healing of Trauma (New York: Penguin Books, 2015).

26. George Orwell, 1984 (Toronto, Ontario: Harper Perennial Classics, 2014).

27. William Shakespeare, The Merchant of Venice (New York ; Toronto: Simon & Schuster Paperbacks, 2010).

28. RAINN, "Victims of Sexual Violence: Statistics," Rainn.org (RAINN, 2020), https://www.rainn.org/statistics/victims-sexual-violence.

29. US Census Bureau, "Census," Census.gov, 2021, https://www.census.gov/.

30. Nick Anderson, Susan Svrluga, and Scout Clement, "Survey Finds Evidence of Widespread Sexual Violence at 33 Universities," Washington Post, October 15, 2019, https://www.washingtonpost.com/local/education/survey-finds-evidence-of-widespread-sexual-violence-at-33-universities/2019/10/14/bd75dcde-ee82-11e9-b648-76bcf86eb67e_story.html.

31. Teresa Wiltz, "Having a Parent behind Bars Costs Children, States," pew.org, May 24, 2016, https://www.pewtrusts.org/en/research-and-analysis/blogs/stateline/2016/05/24/having-a-parent-behind-bars-costs-children-states.

32. Child Trends, "Children's Exposure to Violence," Child Trends, 2017, https://www.childtrends.org/indicators/childrens-exposure-to-violence.

33. Substance Abuse and Mental Health Data Archive. "Survey on Drug Use and Health." SAMHDA, 1996, https://datafiles.samhsa.gov/dataset/national-household-survey-drug-abuse-1996-nhsda-1996-ds0001

34. Eric Anderson, "Five Myths about Cheating," Washington Post, February 13, 2012, sec. Opinions, https://www.washingtonpost.com/opinions/five-myths-about-cheating/2012/02/08/gIQANGdaBR_story.html.

35. Lucille Clifton, "Lucille Clifton Quotation." Assessed 1 June 2021 AZQuotes, www.azquotes.com/quote/486430.

36. Ann Aguirre, Grimspace (New York: Ace Books, 2008).

37. Jean Ferris, Once upon a Marigold (Boston: Sandpiper, 2013).

38. Elwood P. Dowd, "Harvey," Universal Pictures, 1950, https://archive.org/details/harvey-1950.

39. "To Kill a Mockingbird," Brentwood Production, 1962, https://www.amazon.com/Kill-Mockingbird-Gregory-Peck/dp/B000ID37RM.

40. Elia Kazan, A Streetcar Named Desire, (Warner Brothers, 1951).

41. Eve Ensler, The Vagina Monologues, 20th Anniversary ed, (New York: Ballatine, 2018).

42. 20th Century Studios, "The Secret Life of Walter Mitty," YouTube, 2013, https://www.youtube.com/watch?v=COUkpbFVXmM.

43. Jim Rohn, Leading an Inspired Life (Niles, Ill.: Nightingale Conant, 1997).

44. Carol Tuttle, Dressing Your Truth: Discover Your Type of Beauty (Sandy, Utah: Live Your Truth Press, 2015).

45. Rainer Maria Rilke, Rilke's Book of Hours : Love Poems to God (New York: Riverhead Books, 2005).

46. F. Scott Fitzgerald, The Great Gatsby (Harmondsworth: Penguin Books, 1925).

47. William Shakespeare, "All the World's a Stage," (1623), https://www.poetryfoundation.org/poems/56966/speech-all-the-worlds-a-stage.

48. Elvis Presley, Elvis: Inspirations, (Kansas City, MO: Andrews McMeel, 2007).

Five: Reflective You

49. Baltasar Gracián Y Morales, The Art of Worldly Wisdom: A Collection of Aphorisms from the Work of Baltasar Gracian (New York: Doubleday/Currency, G, 1992).

50. Socrates, "Quote," www.goodreads.com, accessed January 11, 2022, https://www.goodreads.com/quotes/748538-the-unexamined-life-is-not-worth-living.

51. James 4:6 (American Standard Version)

52. John Dewey, "The Nature of Freedom." Experience and Education (New York, Macmillan, 1938).

53. Seamus Heaney, Personal Helicon (London: Faber And Faber, 1996).

54. "Coda." The Wonder Years, Season 2, Episode 7, (Beth Rooney, 1989).
55. Charles Bukowski, War All the Time (New York: Harpercollins E-Books, 2009).
56. Stanford University, "When Thomas Jefferson Penned 'All Men Are Created Equal,' He Did Not Mean Individual Equality, Says Stanford Scholar," news.stanford.edu, July 1, 2020, https://news.stanford.edu/press-releases/2020/07/01/meaning-declaratnce-changed-time/.
57. Joseph Campbell, The Hero with a Thousand Faces, Bollingen Series XVII, (Princeton UP, 1972).

Six: Blessed You

58. Willie Nelson with Turk Pipkin, The Tao of Willie: A Guide to the Happiness in Your Heart, (New York: Gotham Books, 2006)
59. Cab Calloway. "Are You Hep to the Jive?" YouTube, uploaded by 1Bluesboy1, 15 Sept. 2008, https://www.youtube.com/watch?v=sgW3RxKdN0Q.
60. Gilbert E. Patterson, "Autobiographia," www.poetrynook.com, 1999, https://www.poetrynook.com/poem/autobiographia.
61. Matthew 7:7 (American Standard Version)
62. Alice Walker, Living by the Word : Essay (San Diego: Harcourt Brace Jovanovich, 1989).
63. 1 Peter 3:9 (American Standard Version)
64. Patrick Kavanagh, "Irish Stew" (London: Martin Brian and O'Keeffe, 1972). 109-110
65. Naomi Shihab Nye, What Have You Lost. (Paw Prints, 2008).
66. C.S Lewis, "Quotation," (Goodreads, 2008), Accessed 1 June 2021. www.goodreads.com/quotes/60537-when-we-lose-one-blessing-another-is-another-is-often-most-unexpectedly.
67. Jalaluddin Rumi, "The Guest House," Rumi: Selected Poems, (Penguin, 2004).
68. Graham Greene, The Honorary Consul (Harmondsworth, England: Penguin, 1973).
69. Mies van der Rohe, (Warburg : Architectural Forum, May 1958)
70. Edwin Markham, "A Creed," www.poetrynook.com, 1901,

https://www.poetrynook.com/poem/creed-1.

71. Thornton Wilder, Our Town : A Play in Three Acts (New York: Perennial, 2003).

Seven: Spiritual You

72. Walt Whitman, www.goodreads.com, accessed January 10, 2022, https://www.goodreads.com/quotes/316394-re-examine-all-you-have-been-told-dismiss-what-insults-your.

73. Pslam 46:10 (American Standard Version)

74. John 1:1 (American Standard Version)

75. Brenda Ueland, "Quotation," www.goodreads.com, accessed January 10, 2022, https://www.goodreads.com/quotes/42295-everyone-is-talented-original-and-has-something-important-to-say.

76. William Shakespeare, Hamlet (Sweden: Wisehouse Classics, 1603).

77. Psalm 139:14 (American Standard Version)

78. Valerie Grant-Sokolosky, Monday Morning Leadership for Women (Dallas, Tx: Cornerstone Leadership Institute, 2004).

79. Carol Tuttle, Dressing Your Truth : Discover Your Type of Beauty (Sandy, Utah: Live Your Truth Press, 2015).

80. Florence Littauer, Personality Plus (Grand Rapids, Mich.: Monarch Books ; Abingdon, U.K, 2007).

81. Paul Laurence Dunbar, "We Wear the Mask," Poetry Foundation, 1895, https://www.poetryfoundation.org/poems/44203/we-wear-the-mask.

82. Joseph Campbell, "A Quote," www.goodreads.com, n.d., https://www.goodreads.com/quotes/192665-the-cave-you-fear-to-enter-holds-the-treasure-you.

83. Isaiah 41:10 (American Standard Version)

84. Jeremiah 46:27 (American Standard Version)

85. 2 Timothy 1:7 (American Standard Version)

86. Matthew 10:31(American Standard Version)

87. Swami Vivekananda, The Complete Works of Swami Vivekananda. (Kolkata: Advaita Ashrama, 2016).

88. Jacques Tourneur, Cat People, Performances by Simone Simon, Tom Conway, and Kent Smith, (RKO Radio Pictures, 1942).

89. William Shakespeare, Hamlet (New York: Simon and Schuster, 2012).

90. Swami Vivekananda, The Complete Works of Swami Vivekananda. (Kolkata: Advaita Ashrama, 2016).

91. John Steinbeck, East of Eden (London: Penguin Books, 2017).

92. Elia Kazan, A Streetcar Named Desire, (Warner Brothers, 1951).

93. Honigsberg, Alexandra E, "Odd Couplets: CPE, Journaling, and Spiritual Poetry." (Journal of Religion and Health, 40.3, 2001, pp. 359+).

Eight: Visionary You

94. Henry David Thoreau, Thoreau's Walden (Camden, Maine: Down East Books, 2019).

95. Eckhart Tolle, The Power of Now: A Guide to Spiritual Enlightenment (Sydney, Nsw: Hachette Australia, 2018).

96. Oprah Winfrey, "A Quote," www.goodreads.com, 1997, https://www.goodreads.com/quotes/625783-create-the-highest-grandest-vision-possible-for-your-life-because.

97. Napoleon Hill, Think and Grow Rich. (1937; repr., S.L.: Simon & Brown, 2019).

98. Rhonda Byrne, The Secret (New York, Ny: Atria Books; Hillsboro, Or, 2016).

99. John 16:23 (American Standard Version)

100. Mark 11:24 (American Standard Version)

101. Matthew 7:7; Luke 11:9 (American Standard Version)

102. Matthew 17:20 (American Standard Version)

103. Mark 6:4 (American Standard Version)

104. Rhonda Byrne, The Secret (New York, Ny: Atria Books; Hillsboro, Or, 2016).

105. Matthew 7:7(American Standard Version)

106. Alice Walker, The Color Purple, (New York: Hartcourt Brace Jovanovich, 1982).

107. Myrna Loy, "Quote," A-Z Quotes, accessed January 10, 2022, https://www.azquotes.com/quote/630968.

108. Proverbs 20:5 (American Standard Version)

109. John Lennon, "Quotes," BrainyQuote, accessed January 10, 2022, https://www.brainyquote.com/quotes/john_lennon_137162.

110. Geoffrey Chaucer, The Canterbury Tales (London: Createspace, 2015).

111. William E. Henley, "Invictus," Poetry Foundation, 2018, https://www.poetryfoundation.org/poems/51642/invictus.

112. Mary Oliver, "The Summer Day," Library of Congress, Washington, D.C. 20540 USA, accessed January 10, 2022, https://www.loc.gov/programs/poetry-and-literature/poet-laureate/poet-laureate-projects/poetry-180/all-poems/item/poetry-180-133/the-summer-day/?__cf_chl_managed_tk__=Swx89QVcQPxDZRaXpeb1jUuv20VG0L_nstP2xjtiZn0-1641797256-0-gaNycGzNCGU.

Nine: Flexible You

113. John F. Kennedy, "Quotation," BrainyQuote (BrainyQuote, 2020), https://www.brainyquote.com/quotes/john_f_kennedy_121068.

114. Shmi Skywalker, "Quote," A-Z Quotes, accessed January 11, 2022, https://www.azquotes.com/quote/1112443.

115. William Shakespeare, Hamlet (Sweden: Wisehouse Classics, 1603).

116. Angelou, Maya. Quotation. *A-Z Quotes*. www.azquotes.com/quote/351342.

117. Shelley, Mary Wollstonecraft, Frankenstein. (Penguin Classics, 2012).

118. Roger Housden, Ten Poems to Say Goodbye (New York: Harmony Books, 2012).

119. William Shakespeare, Hamlet (Sweden: Wisehouse Classics, 1603).

120. J.K. Rowling, "Quote," www.goodreads.com, accessed January 10, 2022,

121. https://www.goodreads.com/quotes/396385-rock-bottom-became-the-solid-foundation-on-which-i-rebuilt.

122. Parker, Garrett. "The Top 20 Richest Authors in the World." MoneyInc., https://moneyinc.com/top-20-richest-authors-world/

123. Henri Matisse, Icarus, 1943-1944, (Scottish National Gallery of Modern Art, Edinburgh).

124. Holy Bible (American Standard Version)

125. Mary Eleanor, New England Nun. (S.L.: Hansebooks, 2017).

126. Charles Darwin, "Quotation," Quoteinvestigator.com, May 4, 2014, https://quoteinvestigator.com/2014/05/04/adapt/.

Ten: Focused You

127. Ralph Marston, "Quotes," BrainyQuote, accessed January 10, 2022, https://www.brainyquote.com/quotes/ralph_marston_564362.

128. Vivekananda, "The Complete Works of Swami Vivekananda."

129. Proverbs 23:7 (American Standard Version)

130. Gerry Robert, The Millionaire Mindset: How Ordinary People Can Create Extraordinary Income (Scottsdale, Az: Lifesuccess Pub, 2007).

131. Zig Ziglar, See You at the Top (Gretna, La.: Pelican Pub, 2013).

132. Martha Beck, "20 Questions That Could Change Your Life," Oprah.com, February 2011, https://www.oprah.com/spirit/martha-becks-20-questions-that-could-change-your-life_1/2

133. "Aristotle's Science of the Best Regime." The American Political Science Review, 1995.

Bibliography

20th Century Studios. "The Secret Life of Walter Mitty." YouTube, 2013.
https://www.youtube.com/watch?v=COUkpbFVXmM.

Aguirre, Ann. *Grimspace*. New York: Berkley, 2008.

Anderson, Eric. "Five Myths about Cheating." *The Washington Post*, 13
Feb. 2012, https://www.washingtonpost.com/opinions/five-myths-
about-cheating/2012/02/08/gIQANGdaBR_story.html.

Anderson, Nick, Susan Svrluga, and Scott Clement. "Survey Finds Evidence
of Widespread Sexual Violence at 33 Universities." *The Washington Post*,
14 Oct. 2019, https://www.washingtonpost.com/local/
education/survey-finds-evidence-of-widespread-sexual-violence-at-33
universities/2019/10/14/bd75dcde-ee82-11e9-b648-
76bcf86eb67e_story.html.

Angelou, Maya. Quotation. *A-Z Quotes*. ww.azquotes.com/quote/351342.

"Aristotle's Science of the Best Regime." The American Political Science
Review 89, no. 1 (1995): 152–60. https://doi.org/10.2307/2083082.

Baltasar, Gracián y Morales. *The Art of Worldly Wisdom*. Boulder:
Shambhala Publications, 2004. p. 39.

Beck, Martha. "Twenty Questions that Could Change Your Life."
Oprah.com, https://www.oprah.com/spirit/martha-becks-20-questions-
that-could-change-your-life_1/all.

Bukowski, Charles. *War All the Time: Poems 1981-1984*. Edited by
Robinson Jeffers. Santa Barbara: Black Sparrow Press, 1984.

Byrne, Rhonda. *The Secret*. New York: Atria Books, 2006.

Calloway, Cab. "Are You Hep to the Jive?" *YouTube*, uploaded by 1Bluesboy1, 15 Sept. 2008, https://www.youtube.com/watch?v=sgW3RxKdN0Q.

Cameron, Julia. *The Artist's Way: A Spiritual Path to Higher Creativity*. Los Angeles: Jeremy P. Torcher/Perigee, 2016.

Campbell, Joseph. *The Hero with a Thousand Faces*. Bollingen Series XVII, Princeton UP, 1972.

Camus, Albert. *Conférences et Discours 1936-1958*. French ed. Paris: Gallimard, 2017.

Canfield, Jack and Janet Switzer. *The Success Principles: How to Get from Where You Are to Where You Want to Be*. New York: HarperCollins, 2005.

Carroll, Latrobe. "Willa Sibert Cather." *Bookman*, May 3, 1921, https://cather.unl.edu/writings/bohlke/interviews/bohlke.i.15

Chaucer, Geoffrey. "Wife of Bath's Tale." *Canterbury Tales*. Included in The *Completed Poetry and Prose of Geoffrey Chaucer*. Edited by John H. Fisher. 2nd ed. Fort Worth: Holt, Rinehart and Winston, 1989, 107-126.

Child Trends. "Children's Exposure to Violence." *Child Trends, 2017* www.childtrends.org/indicators/childrens-exposure-to-violence. Accessed 27 Oct. 2020.

Cisneros, Sandra. *The House on Mango Street*. London: Bloomsbury, 2004.

Clifton, Lucille. "Lucille Clifton Quotation." *AZQuotes*, www.azquotes.com/quote/486430. Assessed 1 June 2021.

"Coda." *The Wonder Years*, Season 2, Episode 7, written by Neal Marlens, Carol Black, and Todd W. Langen, directed by Beth Hillshafer (Beth Rooney), 1989.

Darwin, Charles. "Quotation." Quoteinvestigator.com, May 4, 2014, https://quoteinvestigator.com/2014/05/04/adapt/

Dewey, John. "The Nature of Freedom." *Experience and Education*. New York, Macmillan, 1938.

Doerr, Harriet. Stones of Ibarra. Kbh.: Gyldendal, 1985.

Dowd, Elwood P. "Harvey." Universal Pictures, 1950. https://archive.org/details/harvey-1950.

Dunbar, Paul Laurence. "The Mask." *The Complete Poems of Paul*

Laurence Dunbar. New York, Dodd, Mead, 2012.

Eleanor, Mary. New England Nun. S.L.: Hansebooks, 2017.

Ensler, Eve. *The Vagina Monologues*. 20th Anniversary ed. New York: Ballatine, 2018.

Ferris, Jean. *Once Upon a Marigold*. New York, Hartcourt Children's Books, 2002.

Fitzgerald, F. Scott. *The Great Gatsby*. New York, Charles Scribner's Sons, 1925.

Gelb, Michael J. *How to Think Like Leonardo da Vinci: Seven Steps to Genius Every Day*. New York: Delecorte Press, 1998.

Goldberg, Natalie. *Writing Down the Bones: Freeing the Writer Within*. Expanded ed. Boston: Shambhala, 2005.

Greene, Graham. The Honorary Consul. Harmondsworth, England: Penguin, 1973.

Haught, Kaylin. "God Says Yes to Me." *The Palm of Your Hand*. Thomaton, ME: Tilbury House Publishers, 1995.

Heaney, Seamus. "Personal Helicon." *Death of a Naturalist*. New York, Farrar, Straus and Giroux, 1966.

Henley, William Ernest. "Invictus." *Book of Verses*. 1875.

Hill, Napoleon. *Think and Grow Rich: The Complete Classic Text*. Deluxe edition, New York, Tarcher Perigee, 2008.

Honigsberg, Alexandra E. "Odd Couplets: CPE, Journaling, and Spiritual Poetry." *Journal of Religion and Health*, 40.3, 2001, pp. 359+.

Housden, Roger. Ten Poems to Say Goodbye. New York: Harmony Books, 2012.

Jim Rohn. Leading an Inspired Life. Niles, Ill.: Nightingale Conant, 1997.

Joyce, James. *Dubliners*. London, Grant Richards Limited, 1914.

Kavanagh, Patrick. "Irish Stew." *Patrick Kavanagh: Collected Poems*. London, Martin Brian and O'Keeffe, 1972. 109-110.

Kaufman, Millard. Bowl of Cherries. London: Atlantic, 2009.

Kazan, Elia, director. *A Streetcar Named Desire*. Performances by Vivien Leigh, Marlon Brando, Kim Hunter, and Karl Malden, Warner Brothers, 1951.

Kennedy, John. *Address in the Assembly Hall at the Paulskirche in Frankfurt*. June 25, 1963, https://www.presidency.uscb.eduddress. Accessed 17 August 2020.

Key, Frances Scott. "The Defense of Fort M'Henry." *American and Commercial Daily Advertiser* (Boston), Approximately Sept. 17, 1812.

Kolk, Bessel van der. The Body Keeps the Score: Brain, Mind and Body in the Healing of Trauma. New York: Penguin Books, 2015.

Koster, Henry, director. *Harvey*. Performances by James Stewart, Josephine Hull, Jesse White, and Charles Drake, Universal, 1950.

L'Amour, Louis. *Education of a Wandering Man: A Memoir*. New York: Bantam Books, 1989.

Lewis, C.S. Quotation. *Goodreads*. 2008, www.goodreads.com/quotes/ 60537-when-we-lose--one-blessing-another-is-another-is-often-most-unexpectedly. Accessed 1 June 2021.

Littauer, Florence. *Personality Plus: How to Understand Others by Understanding Yourself*. Grand Rapids, Revell, 1992.

Lowe, Janet, editor. *Oprah Winfrey Speaks: Insight from the World's Most Influential Voice*. New York, John Wiley and Sons, 1998.

Loy, Myrna. "Quote." A-Z Quotes. Accessed January 10, 2022. https://www.azquotes.com/quote/630968.

Markham, Edwin. "A Creed." www.poetrynook.com, 1901.

Marston, Ralph. Quotation. A-Z Quotes, https://www.azquotes.com/ author/19649-Ralph_Marston/tag/inspirational. Accessed 1 June 2021.

Matisse, Henri. *Icarus*. 1943-1944, Scottish National Gallery of Modern Art, Edinburgh.

Mies van der Rohe, Warburg. *Architectural Forum*. May 1958.

Nelson, Willie with Turk Pipkin. *The Tao of Willie: A Guide to the Happiness in Your Heart*. New York, Gotham Books, 2006.

Nin, Anaïs. "The New Woman." *Ramparts Magazine* (June 1974): 42-44. https://www.unz.com/print/Ramparts-1974jun-00037/

Nye, Naomi Shihab, ed. *What Have You Lost?* New York, HarperCollins, 1999.

O'Connor, Flannery. "Quotation." www.goodreads.com, n.d. https://www.goodreads.com/quotes/315733-i-write-because-i-don-t-know-what-i-think-until.

Oliver, Mary. "The Summer Day." *Devotion*. New York, Random House, 2017. p. 316.

Orwell, George. *1984*. London, Secker and Warburg, 1949.

Parker, Garrett. "The Top 20 Richest Authors in the World." *MoneyInc.*, https://moneyinc.com/top-20-richest-authors-world/

Patterson, G.E. "Autobiographia." *Tug*. Minneapolis, Graywolf Press, 1999.

Presley, Elvis. *Elvis: Inspirations,* Mike Evans, ed. Kansas City, MO, Andrews McMeel, 2007.

Racine, Jean. *Britannicus.* 1669. French Edition. Paris: Librairie Larousse, 1964.

Rainer Maria Rilke. *Rilke's Book of Hours: Love Poems to God*. New York: Riverhead Books, 2005.

Robert, Gerry. *The Millionaire Mindset: How Ordinary People Can Create Extraordinary Income*. Scottsdale, Az: Lifesuccess Pub, 2007.

Rowling, J.K. "Quote." www.goodreads.com. Accessed January 10, 2022. https://www.goodreads.com/quotes/396385-rock-bottom-became-the-solid-foundation-on-which-i-rebuilt.

Rumi, Jalaluddin. "Guest House." *Rumi: Selected Poems*. Translated by Coleman BarksBooks, 2004 with John Moynce, A.J. Arberry, Reynold Nicholson, Penguin, 2004.

Shakespeare, William. *Hamlet*. Updated edition, Folger Shakespeare Library, Edited by Barbara A. Mowat and Werstine, New York, Simon and Schuster, 2012.

Shakespeare, William. *The Merchant of Venice.* Floyd, VA, Wilder Publications, 2014.

Shelley, Mary Wollstonecraft. *Frankenstein*. Penguin Classics. 2012.

Skywalker, Shmi. "Quote." A-Z Quotes. Accessed January 11, 2022. https://www.azquotes.com/quote/1112443.

Socrates. "Quote." www.goodreads.com. Accessed January 11, 2022. https://www.goodreads.com/quotes/748538-the-unexamined-life-is-not-worth-living.

Sokolosky, Valerie. *Monday Morning Leadership for Women*. Dallas, Cornerstone Leadership for Women, 2004.

Substance Abuse and Mental Health Data Archive. "Survey on Drug Use and Health." *SAMHDA*, 1996, https://datafiles.samhsa.gov/dataset/national -household-survey-drug-abuse-1996-nhsda-1996-ds0001. 31 May 2021.

Stanford University. "When Thomas Jefferson Penned 'All Men Are Created Equal,' He Did Not Mean Individual Equality, Says Stanford

Scholar." news.stanford.edu, July 1, 2020.
https://news.stanford.edu/press-releases/2020/07/01/meaning-declaratnce-changed-time/

St. James, Simone. *The Broken Girls*. New York: Berkley, 2018.

Steinbeck, John. *East of Eden*. Middlesex, England, Penguin, 1952.

Stevens, Wallace. "Thirteen Ways of Looking at a Blackbird." poets.org, 1954. https://poets.org/poem/thirteen-ways-looking-blackbird.

Thomas, Dylan. "Do Not Go Gentle into That Good Night." *The Poems of Dylan Thomas*. New York, New Directions, 1953.

Thoreau, Henry David. *Walden*. Black and White Classics, 2014.

Tolle, Eckhart. *The Power of Now: A Guide to Spiritual Enlightenment*. Novato, CA, Namaste Publishing and New World Library, 1999.

Tourneur, Jacques, director. *Cat People*. Performances by Simone Simon, Tom Conway, and Kent Smith, RKO Radio Pictures, 1942.

Tuttle, Carol. *It's Just My Nature: A Guide to Knowing and Living Your True Nature*. 2nd edition, Live Your Truth Press, 2015.

2018 U.S. Census. *United States Census Bureau*, 2021, https://www.census.gov/. 31 May 2021.

Ueland, Brenda. *If You Want to Write: A Book about Art, Independence and Spirit*. 2nd edition, Saint Paul, Graywolf Press, 1987.

"Victims of Sexual Violence: Statistics." *Rape, Abuse, and Incest National Network (RAINN)*, 2021, https://www.rainn.org/statistics/victims-sexual-violence. Accessed 11 Nov. 2021.

Walker, Alice. *The Color Purple*. New York, Hartcourt Brace Jovanovich, 1982.

Walker, Alice. *Living by the Word: Selected Writings 1973-1987*. San Diego, Harcourt Brace Jovanovich, 1988.

Wallas, Graham. *The Art of Thought*. London: Jonathan Cape, 1926.

Whitman, Walt. *Leaves of Grass and Selected Prose*. Edited by Sculley Bradley, New York, Holt, Rinehart and Winston, 1949.

Wilder, Thornton. *Our Town: A Play in Three Acts*. New York, Perennial Classics, 2003.

Wiltz, Teresa. "Having a Parent Behind Bars Costs Children, States." *PEW: Stateline*, 24 May 2016, https://www.pewtrusts.org/en/research-and-analysis/blogs/stateline/2016/05 /24/having-a-parent-behind-bars-costs-children-states. Accessed 17 July 2021.

Winfrey, Oprah. "A Quote." www.goodreads.com, 1997. https://www.goodreads.com/quotes/625783-create-the-highest-grandest-vision-possible-for-your-life-because.

Ziglar, Zig. *See You at the Top.* New Orleans, Pelican, 2010. p. 166.